George Washington Moon

**Ecclesiastical English**

A Series of Criticisms Showing the Old Testament Revisers' Violations of the Laws of

the Language

George Washington Moon

**Ecclesiastical English**

*A Series of Criticisms Showing the Old Testament Revisers' Violations of the Laws of the Language*

ISBN/EAN: 9783337084660

Printed in Europe, USA, Canada, Australia, Japan

Cover: Foto ©Thomas Meinert / pixelio.de

More available books at **www.hansebooks.com**

# ECCLESIASTICAL ENGLISH:

## A SERIES OF CRITICISMS

*SHOWING THE OLD TESTAMENT REVISERS' VIOLATIONS OF THE LAWS OF THE LANGUAGE,*

ILLUSTRATED BY MORE THAN 1000 QUOTATIONS.

(BEING PART II OF 'THE REVISERS' ENGLISH'.)

BY

G. WASHINGTON MOON, Hon. F.R.S.L.

*Author of 'The Dean's English', &c.*

" The care bestowed upon language is bestowed on the most perfect instrument of the mind, without which all other gifts are valueless."—
THE EDINBURGH REVIEW.

LONDON
HATCHARDS, PUBLISHERS, 187, PICCADILLY.

1886.

# Dedication.

I dedicate these Criticisms to one whose many excellencies endear him to the mightiest in the land, and whose additional commendation to me is his mastery over the English language. The purity of his diction, the felicity of his expressions, and the gracefulness of his style, are unsurpassed by those of any other of my literary correspondents.

DEDICATED TO

SIR *ANDREW CLARK,* BART.,

M.D., LL.D., F.R.S., F.R.C.P., &c.

# PREFACE.

The recent Revision of the Sacred Scriptures occupied the most illustrious English scholars nearly fifteen years; and such was the anticipated extent of the sale of the work, that the quantity of paper ordered for the edition was so enormous, that had the sheets been piled one upon another in reams as they left the mill, it was said that they would have formed a column ten times the height of St. Paul's Cathedral; or, had they been made into a strip six inches wide, it would have been sufficient with which to "put a girdle round the world"! Yet, within a few months of the issuing of that stupendous work, the great excitement which had heralded and accompanied its publication, died down; and so cooled became the once glowing ardour of the booksellers who, under its influence, had been induced to make excessive purchases, that they were offering their surplus copies at less than half price,—and offering them in vain.

Englishmen had long regarded their Bible as the "well of English undefiled"; and many of them, when speaking of the then forthcoming Revision of the Sacred Scriptures, seemed, by their enthusiasm, to believe that, under the mighty influence of those learned Doctors, a miracle would be wrought, as of old, and the water of this well would, as it were, be changed into wine. Was there ever so joyful an anticipation of a rich draught of delight so cruelly mocked as was this one by the discovery of the lamentable emptiness of the *fiasco?* There was no wine in the cup; and even the water from the old well was found, upon examination, to be charged with effete matter.

But, whence was the bitterness of this disappointment—the source of this *Marah?* It sprang from the ignorance of those who had entertained the sanguine belief respecting the wonders to be wrought by the Revisers. Those persons little knew the nature of the education of the men who had been born in the early part of the present century. *In those days the study of English was utterly ignored in the higher Schools and Colleges of the land.* The writer gladly recognises the vast stores of learning possessed by the Revisers, and joins his countrymen in acknowledging the debt of gratitude due to those eminent scholars for so generously devoting their time and talents to the accomplishment of the great work. They did their duty nobly to the best of their ability, but they had not made English their study. What wonder, then, is it that their work is not characterized by purity of diction or elegance of style?

To say that there are errors in it, that those errors are gross, that their grossness is flagrant, and that they abound throughout the work, is indeed a grave charge to bring against it; but, in the interests of our language, it must be brought; and the gravity of the charge is the greater because of its transparent truth.

But gross, and flagrant, and abounding as are the errors, they would be freely pardoned had they been made by uneducated men. The *gravamen* is that the work, with all its faults, has gone forth to the world as the result of years of combined effort of England's most illustrious scholars! And if the present state of our language—a language glorified by being the vehicle for conveying to mankind the sublime thoughts of Milton and of Shakspeare —be judged by the English of the Revisers, the world's unfaltering verdict upon it must be "Ichabod! Ichabod!"

And shall we, by our silence, pardonable though it would be as emanating from respect to the Revisers, allow their English to be accepted as the accredited evidence of the accuracy, gracefulness, and strength to which our language has attained? The proud love which we cherish for our language impels us to say No!

But, even were Englishmen willing to be silent, sooner or later the truth would declare itself, and reveal to the world that a sacred trust having been committed to the Revisers to translate the Divine Records into faultless English based on the time-hallowed version of 1611, the Revisers, instead of making the Scriptures a model of excellence—the language worthy of the thoughts that it conveyed—had given to the English-speaking peoples a work marred by violations of grammar, ungracefulness of style, and infelicities of expression, all evidencing but too plainly that however learned the Revisers were in the classic languages of antiquity, they were not masters of their own mother tongue. In this sweeping charge, the writer does not wholly include the American Revisers. They suggested many great improvements which were not carried out by their English collaborators, with whom rested the final decision in all matters.

The reader will find in these pages a truthful exposure of the Revisers' most glaring errors of language, with chapter and verse for every quotation, so that the accuracy of the writer's statements may be tested. Were he not able thus to challenge investigation of the charges which he brings against the Revisers, he would shrink from publishing these criticisms, for he is certain that this work would not be received as truthful; so difficult would it be to believe that such errors had been committed by such men.*

The task has not been an enviable one; but no man should shrink from the performance of obvious duty. The exposure had to be made, and the writer has made it; and he trusts that in so doing he has rendered some slight service to all students of the language.

As for the work itself, he hopes that at some future time his labours will be useful to those who will not merely undertake the revision of the Sacred Scriptures, but will faithfully accomplish that which they undertake, and make the Word of God, what the writer has always contended that it should be, THE EMBODIMENT OF THE PUREST TRUTH IN THE PUREST LANGUAGE.

*London*, 1886.

---

* "The Revised Old Testament represents the result of the patient deliberation of the best scholars of the whole English-speaking world."—*The Church Quarterly Review, July,* 1885, *p.* 442.

# THE OLD TESTAMENT REVISERS,
## 1870—1885.

ALEXANDER, Dr. W. L. .........Professor of Theology, Congregational Church Hall, Edinburgh.
BENSLY, Mr. R. L. ...............Fellow of Caius College, Cambridge.
BIRRELL, Rev. J...................Professor of Oriental Languages, St. Andrews.
BROWNE, Dr. HAROLD .........Bishop of Ely.
CHANCE, Dr. F. ....................Fellow of Trinity College, Cambridge.
CHENERY, Mr. T....................Lord Almoner's Professor of Arabic, Oxford.
CHEYNE, Dr. T. K. ...............Fellow of Balliol College, Oxford.
COOK, Rev. F. C. ..................Canon of Exeter.
DAVIDSON, Dr. A. B. ............Professor of Hebrew, Free Church College, Edinburgh.
DAVIES, Dr. B......................Professor of Hebrew, Baptist College, Regent's Park, London.
DOUGLAS, Dr. .....................Professor of Hebrew, Free Church College, Glasgow.

## LIST OF REVISERS.

DRIVER, Dr. .........................Regius Professor of Hebrew, Oxford.
ELLIOTT, Rev. C. J.................Formerly Fellow of St. Catharine's College, Cambridge.
FAIRBAIRN, Dr. P. ...............Principal of the Free Church, Glasgow.
FIELD, Dr. F. ......................Formerly Fellow of Trinity College, Cambridge.
GEDEN, Mr. J. D...................Professor of Hebrew, Wesleyan College, Didsbury.
GINSBURG, Dr. CHRISTIAN D...Editor of *"The Massorah"*, &c.
GOTCH, Dr. F. W...................Principal of the Baptist College, Bristol.
HARRISON, Rev. B. ...............Archdeacon of Maidstone.
HERVEY, Lord ARTHUR.........Bishop of Bath and Wells.
JEBB, Dr. JOHN ...................Canon of Hereford.
KAY, Dr. WILLIAM ...............Honorary Canon of St. Albans.
LEATHES, Rev. STANLEY ......Professor of Hebrew, King's College, London.
LUMBY, Dr. .........................Norrisian Professor of Divinity, Cambridge.
McGILL, Rev. J. ...................Professor of Oriental Languages, St. Andrews.
OLLIVANT, Dr. .....................Bishop of Llandaff.
PEROWNE, Dr. J. J. S. .........Dean of Peterborough.
PLUMPTRE, Dr......................Dean of Wells.
PUSEY, Dr. .........................Regius Professor of Hebrew, Oxford.

## LIST OF REVISERS.   xiii.

ROSE, Archdeacon ...............
SAYCE, Rev. A. H. ...............Deputy Professor of Comparative Philology, Oxford.
SELWYN, Professor...............
SMITH, Dr. PAYNE ...............Dean of Canterbury.
SMITH, Dr. W. ROBERTSON ...Professor of Hebrew in the Free Church, Aberdeen.
THIRLWALL, Dr. ..................Bishop of St. David's.
WEIR, Dr. D. H. ...............Professor of Oriental Languages, Glasgow.
WORDSWORTH, Dr. ...............Bishop of Lincoln.
WRIGHT, Dr. W. ...............Professor of Arabic, Cambridge.

Of the above, Dr. Pusey and Canon Cook declined to serve; the Bishop of Lincoln and Dr. Jebb soon withdrew; and somewhat later Dr. Plumptre resigned.

The following members died during the progress of the work:—Mr. Chenery, Dr. B. Davies, Rev. C. J. Elliott, Dr. P. Fairbairn, Rev. J. McGill, Dr. Ollivant, Archdeacon Rose, Professor Selwyn, Dr. Thirlwall, and Dr. D. H. Weir. And Dr. W. L. Alexander and Dr. F. Field died during the interval between the completion and the publication of the work.

The Secretary to the Old Testament Company was Mr. W. Aldis Wright, Fellow of Trinity College, Cambridge.

The Company was strengthened by the coöperation of the American Revisers; as was also the New Testament Company.

# CONTENTS.

## A.

'A' or 'an' ......27, 63–70, 96, 101
Adjectives and adverbs 112, 116
'Afore' and 'before'... 15
'After',–'according to' 157
'Afterward' and 'afterwards' ............138, 139
'Again' .........76–78, 211
Agur...................... 129
Aha! for Ha, ha! ...... 210
All *of you*...............87, 88
'Also', redundant ...... 92
'Alway' and 'always' 138
'Am', the verb '*to am*' 103
Ambiguity .........162, 163
Angels 'ascending and descending' ......... 49
'Annul' and 'disannul' 30, 31
'Another', for 'the other' ...............97–99
'Apparalled', for 'clothed' 18, 19
'Are' and 'be' ...103–107
A son of man ............ 100
'As—as', and 'so—as' 151–154
Assembled together ... 80
'Astonied' and 'astonished' ...............15, 16
'Attired' and 'tired'... 22
'Aught' and 'ought'... 16
'Augmenteth', for 'increaseth' ............... 19
Avenged *of*, for *on*...... 123

## B.

'Back' and 'backward' 28
'Backward' and 'backwards' ................... 139
Baker's '*Remarks on English*' ............... 1
Bath and Wells, Bishop of ........................ 11
Be, the verb 'to be'.. 103–107, 154
'Before' and 'afore'... 15
'Beside' and 'besides' 132–136
Bible, the 'Temple of Truth' ............213–215
Black and white identical ..................... 29
Blackness and paleness 28
Bloomed blossoms ... 79

## CONTENTS.

| | Page |
|---|---|
| 'Both', redundant | 85 |
| Both *of them* | 87–89 |
| Both of those—right | 89, 90 |
| Brass, a natural product | 209 |
| 'Bridles' for 'bits' | 209 |
| Broken hearted | 17 |
| Budded buds | 99 |
| 'Builded' and 'built' | 14 |
| 'But', the meaning of | 85, 86 |
| 'But' redundant | 86 |
| 'But', for 'that' | 85 |

### C.

| | |
|---|---|
| 'Cankerworm' | 17 |
| 'Chiefest' | 27 |
| 'Clothed' and 'apparalled' | 18, 19 |
| Collocation of words | 52 |
| Colour, non-existent | 29 |
| Comma, its importance | 212 |
| '*Common Errors in Speaking and Writing*' | 33 |
| Compound words | 17, 18 |
| 'Congregation', singular and plural | 39 |
| Convocation's vote of thanks | 5 |
| Corpses, live and dead | 212 |
| Cowper quoted | 35 |
| 'Cry with my voice' | 80 |

### D.

| | Page |
|---|---|
| Darwinism | 29 |
| 'Dead body that is dead' | 79 |
| Dead corpses | 212 |
| 'Deceased' for 'dead' | 18 |
| 'Depart *away*' | 85 |
| 'Descending' and 'ascending' | 49 |
| 'Despite' | 123 |
| 'Devised devices' | 80 |
| 'Diminished' and 'minished' | 20 |
| 'Disannul' and 'annul' | 30, 31 |
| 'Doubled' twice | 77 |
| 'Downward' and 'downwards' | 139 |
| 'Drave' and 'drove' | 15 |
| 'Dwelled' and 'dwelt' | 15 |

### E.

| | |
|---|---|
| Each *of them* | 87, 88 |
| Each one | 148 |
| 'Eagle', for 'eagle's' | 210 |
| Earth, neuter and feminine | 30 |
| 'Eat' and 'eat up' | 148 |
| '*Edinburgh Review.*' | 10 |
| 'Either', for 'each' | 144, 145 |
| 'Else but', for 'else than' | 91 |

## CONTENTS. xvii.

| | Page |
|---|---|
| 'Else save', for 'else than' | 91 |
| Emphasis, the place of | 55, 62 |
| End, no or none | 70 |
| Errors, cause of the Revisers' | 102 |
| 'Established' and 'stablished' | 19, 20 |
| Esther, Queen | 127 |
| Eunuch, a or an | 69, 70 |
| 'Ever' and 'never' | 161 |
| 'Ever and ever' | 176 |
| 'Every drove by *themselves*' | 143 |
| 'Every man by *their* families' | 144 |
| 'Exceeding' for 'exceedingly' | 115, 116 |
| 'Exceeding magnifical' | 116 |
| 'Except', for 'unless' | 205–207 |
| 'Expended' | 7 |
| Eye, no or none | 70 |

### F.

| | |
|---|---|
| Feet, stood on | 79 |
| 'Firstripe' | 17 |
| 'For' before infinitives | 117–119 |
| 'For ever' | 78 |
| 'For', redundant | 119 |

| | Page |
|---|---|
| 'Forward' and 'forwards' | 139 |

### G.

| | |
|---|---|
| Garment, an hairy | 27 |
| 'Gathered to his fathers' | 28 |
| 'Gathered up his feet' | 28 |
| German revision of Luther's Bible | 12 |
| Gift, to take | 28 |
| 'Good English' | 11 |
| Grammar, the Revisers' | 32 |
| 'Grapegatherers' | 17 |

### H.

| | |
|---|---|
| H, a and an before | 63–67 |
| H, my and mine before | 63, 73, 74 |
| H, thy and thine before | 64, 72 |
| Ha, ha! or aha! | 210 |
| 'Had rather be' | 190 |
| 'Hairy' and ''airy' | 68 |
| Hairy garment, an | 27 |
| Hairy man, a | 27, 68 |
| Hairy man, an | 27, 68 |
| Hairy mantle, a | 27 |
| Half, 'one half' | 148 |
| Handmaids | 30 |
| 'Hardly', its two meanings | 25 |
| 'Harlots unto the King' | 53 |

## CONTENTS.

'Heard with our ears'. 80
'Heart deceitful above all things' ............ 129
'Heavier than *them*' .. 213
Hebrew language ...... 76
'Hence' and 'from hence' ............... 74–176
Hermaphroditos ...... 30
Hiatus ................... 69
'Homer' or 'omer' ... 26
Honour .................. 74

### I.

'If' and 'though' ...... 205
'If', for 'whether' ... 205
'In' and 'on' ............. 122
'In', for 'into' ...... 119–121
'In' or 'on' ............. 61
Inconsistency ...9, 26, 112
'Increaseth' and 'augmenteth' ............. 19
Infinitive past, for present .................... 7
Inhabitant, no and none 71
'Inward' and 'inwards' ................... 139
ἱστορία ................ 14
'Its', date of introduction into Bible ...... 208

### J.

Joash and Jehoash...... 201
Joahaz and Jehoahaz... 201
Journey, to take......... 28

### K.

Kneeling on his knees. 79
Knowledge and wisdom ...................... 35

### L.

'Last end' ................ 95
Latinisms ................ 18
'Latter end' ............. 95
'Let', its two meanings ...................... 22
'Lettan', to hinder ... 22
Levins, Peter, quoted . 14
Levity ..................... 68
'Look sad' and 'look sadly' ................... 114
Lightning and thunder 48
Live corpses ............ 212
'Lœtan' to loose ...... 22
'Loose' and 'unloose'. 31
Lowth, Bishop, quoted 1

### M.

Maacah, Rehoboam's wife ...................... 128
Maids ..................... 30
Man, a or an hairy ... 27
'*Manipulus Vocabulorum*' .................. 14
Mantle, a hairy ......... 27
'Minished' and 'diminished' ............. 20
Mood, subjunctive 107–111

## CONTENTS. xix.

| | Page |
|---|---|
| Moses, meeker than all men | 127 |
| Multitude, noun of | 6 |
| 'Multitude', singular or plural | 39 |

### N.

| | Page |
|---|---|
| 'Naught' and 'nought' | 16 |
| 'Naughty' and 'noughty' | 16 |
| 'Never', for 'ever' | 161 |
| 'Nitre', for 'natron' | 208 |
| 'No end' and 'none end' | 70 |
| 'No eye' and 'none eye' | 70 |
| 'No inhabitant' and 'none inhabitant' | 71 |
| 'No—nor' | 159 |
| 'No—or' | 159 |
| 'No' or 'not' | 154, 155 |
| 'None' and 'no one' | 71 |
| 'None other' and 'no other' | 131 |
| 'None', singular or plural | 71 |
| 'Not—nor' | 156 |
| 'Not—or' | 156 |
| Noun of multitude | 6 |

### O.

| | |
|---|---|
| 'O' and 'Oh' | 201–204 |
| Of; 'all of', 'both of', 'each of' | 87, 147 |
| 'Of', for 'by', for 'on' for 'with' | 122, 213 |
| 'Of', omitted | 124, 125 |
| 'Of', redundant | 124 |
| 'Of them', redundant | 161 |
| 'Omer' or 'homer' | 26 |
| One; 'each one' | 148 |
| 'One half' | 148 |
| Oneness of all animals | 29 |
| Oneness of all colours | 29 |
| One; 'such a one', or 'such an one' | 70 |
| Other; 'none or no' | 131 |
| 'Other', omitted | 126, 130 |
| 'Other', redundant | 130, 132 |
| 'Outward' and 'outwards' | 139 |
| 'Ought' and 'aught' | 16 |

### P.

| | |
|---|---|
| Pale, waxed | 28, 29 |
| 'Parted them both asunder' | 85 |
| Participle, present for past | 7 |
| Past infinitive, for present | 7–10 |
| 'People of his pasture' | 201 |
| 'People', singular or plural | 37, 38 |
| 'Peoples' | 39, 40 |
| 'Persons' | 39, 40 |
| Perspicuity | 52 |

|  | Page |
|---|---|
| 'Pitched with pitch' | 79 |
| 'Plain' or 'plainly' | 112, 115 |
| 'Plaistered with plaister' | 79 |
| Positive assertions, weak | 175, 176 |
| 'Praying a prayer' | 79 |
| 'Precede' or 'prevent' | 22 |
| Prepositions | 122 |
| 'Prevent' | 121 |
| '*Probe-bibel*' | 12 |
| Pronouns, ambiguous | 162, 163 |
| Pronouns, errors in | 167, 173 |
| Pronouns, redundant | 83, 92–94 |
| Pronouns, relative | 164–166 |
| 'Pruninghooks' | 17 |

### R.

|  |  |
|---|---|
| Rams' skins | 18 |
| Rather; 'had rather be' | 190 |
| Redundancy | 75–82 |
| Rise *up* | 84 |

### S.

|  |  |
|---|---|
| 'Sarai Abraham's wife' | 211 |
| Saxon words | 18 |
| Sea, masculine, feminine and neuter | 30 |
| Seal skins | 18 |

|  | Page |
|---|---|
| Second times, two | 212 |
| 'See it with thine eyes' | 80 |
| Sequence of words | 47–60, 183, 190–193 |
| Shakspeare quoted | 23 |
| 'Shall' and 'will' | 177–182 |
| 'Sheep of his hand' | 210 |
| 'Sick *of* love' | 212, 213 |
| Smith, John, his book | 174 |
| 'So—as' and as—as' | 151–154 |
| Solomon wiser than all men | 126 |
| Somersetshire witness | 163 |
| 'Son of man' | 100 |
| 'Speak plain', or 'plainly' | 112, 113 |
| 'Spite' and 'despite' | 123 |
| 'Stablished' and 'established' | 20 |
| Stargazers | 17 |
| 'Stole' and 'stole away' | 28 |
| 'Stone him with stones' | 82, 83 |
| 'Stood up on his feet' | 79 |
| 'Storehouse' | 17 |
| 'Storeys' and 'stories' | 14 |
| 'Stories' in the ark | 14 |
| 'Strewed', 'strawed' or 'strowed' | 26 |
| 'Stronghold' and 'strong hold' | 17 |

# CONTENTS.

|  | Page |
|---|---|
| Subjunctive mood | 107–111, 183 |
| 'Such *a* one' and 'such *an* one' | 70 |
| Swallowed 'up' and 'down' | 149, 150 |

### T.

| | |
|---|---|
| Take, a gift and a journey | 28 |
| Tautology | 10, 75–82 |
| 'Tell', to count | 23, 24 |
| Temple of Truth, the Bible | 213–215 |
| Tentative Edition of Revision | 12 |
| 'Than' | 132 |
| 'Than them' | 213 |
| 'The', 'a', or 'an' | 96, 97 |
| 'Thee', for 'thou' | 170, 186 |
| 'Them' and 'those' | 172 |
| 'Thence' and 'from thence' | 194–196 |
| 'The son of man', for '*a* son of man' | 100 |
| 'This' and 'that' | 200 |
| 'This twenty years' and 'these twenty years' | 141 |
| 'Though', for 'if' | 205 |
| 'Thunder and lightning' | 48 |

| | Page |
|---|---|
| 'Thy' and 'thine' | 72 |
| 'Tidings', singular and plural | 43 |
| 'Time past' and 'times past' | 139 |
| *Times, The*, quoted | 5, 13 |
| 'Tired' and 'attired' | 22 |
| 'Tired wheels' | 22 |
| 'To' and 'unto' | 121 |
| Tongue, 'in' or 'on' the | 61 |
| 'Toward' and 'towards' | 139 |

### U.

| | |
|---|---|
| 'Unless' and 'except' | 205–207 |
| 'Unloose' and 'loose' | 31 |
| 'Unto' and 'to' | 121 |
| Up; 'eat up' | 148, 149 |
| Up; 'swallowed up' | 149, 150 |
| 'Upward' and 'upwards' | 139 |

### V.

| | |
|---|---|
| Vacillation of the Revisers | 137 |
| 'Vanish *away*' | 84 |
| Verb, its primary importance | 32 |

Verbs, errors in...33, 41–49, 183–189
'Vomit them up *again*' 78
Vote of thanks to the Revisers ............... 6

## W.

'Waxed pale' .........28, 29
Weighed out, 'expended' ............... 7
'Weight...in weight'. 10
'Whence' and 'from whence'............194–196
'Whether' and 'if' ... 205
'Which', for 'who' ... 10
'While' and 'whiles'.. 141
'Who' and 'which' 164–166

Whom; 'the man's rod *whom*' .................. 173
'Will' and 'shall'... 177–182
'Wilt', for 'willest'... 204
'Widow *woman*' ...... 81
'Wisdom' and 'knowledge' .................. 35
Wisdom, its existence ignored ............... 36
'Women servants' ... 30
'Wonderful great' ... 116

## Y.

Years, 'this twenty' and 'these twenty'. 141
'You' and 'ye' ...166, 170
Youth, 'like an eagle'. 210

# INDEX OF TEXTS.

## GENESIS.

| Chap. | Ver. | Page. |
|---|---|---|
| ii. | 15 | 118 |
|  | 17 | 76 |
|  | 18 | 65 |
|  | 29 | 65 |
|  | 21 | 162 |
| iii. | 6 | 118 |
| iv. | 2 | 211 |
|  | 12 | 30 |
|  | 13 | 179 |
|  | 14 | 179 |
|  | 17 | 162 |
|  | 22 | 124 |
| vi. | 5 | 122 |
|  | 6 | 122 |
|  | 7 | 89 |
|  | 13 | 122 |
|  | 14 | 79 |
|  | 16 | 13 |
|  | 17 | 56, 122 |
| vii. | 21 | 90 |
| viii. | 3 | 65 |
|  | 8 | 204 |
|  | 10 | 130 |
|  | 20 | 14 |
| ix. | 20 | 65 |
| xii. | 12 | 179 |
|  | 17 | 210, 211 |
| xiii. | 12 | 15 |
|  | 18 | 14, 15 |

## Genesis—(con.)

| Chap. | Ver. | Page. |
|---|---|---|
| xv. | 1 | 115 |
|  | 9 | 65 |
|  | 10 | 98 |
| xvi. | 1 | 65, 210, 211 |
| xvii. | 6 | 115 |
| xviii. | 2 | 183 |
|  | 21 | 205 |
| xix. | 12 | 134 |
| xx. | 1 | 196 |
| xxi. | 16 | 183 |
| xxii. | 4 | 183 |
|  | 6 | 88 |
|  | 8 | 88 |
| xxiii. | 6 | 86 |
| xxiv. | 11 | 118 |
|  | 23 | 76 |
| xxv. | 25 | 27, 68 |
| xxvi. | 1 | 135 |
|  | 17 | 196 |
|  | 22 | 196 |
| xxvii. | 11 | 27, 68 |
|  | 21 | 155 |
| xxviii. | 12 | 49 |
|  | 17 | 130 |
| xxix. | 4 | 106 |
| xxxi. | 18 | 117 |
|  | 19 | 28 |
|  | 20 | 28 |
|  | 38 | 141 |

## INDEX OF TEXTS.

### Genesis—(con.)

| Chap. | Ver. | Page. |
|---|---|---|
| xxxi. | 41 | 142 |
|  | 42 | 205 |
|  | 46 | 65 |
|  | 49 | 98 |
|  | 50 | 135 |
| xxxii. | 16 | 143 |
|  | 22 | 30 |
|  | 26 | 205 |
| xxxiii. | 11 | 28 |
|  | 12 | 28 |
|  | 17 | 65 |
| xxxiv. | 12 | 161 |
|  | 15 | 106 |
|  | 22 | 106 |
|  | 30 | 177 |
|  | 31 | 65 |
| xxxvi. | 15 | 113 |
|  | 43 | 106 |
| xxxvii. | 14 | 205 |
|  | 32 | 154 |
| xxxix. | 5 | 55 |
|  | 6 | 55 |
| xl. | 7 | 114 |
|  | 10 | 205 |
|  | 13 | 72 |
|  | 19 | 72 |
|  | 21 | 76 |
| xli. | 32 | 77 |
|  | 48 | 36 |
|  | 57 | 117 |
| xlii. | 7 | 117, 196 |
|  | 13 | 183 |
|  | 15 | 205 |
|  | 32 | 183 |

### Genesis—(con.)

| Chap. | Ver. | Page. |
|---|---|---|
| xliii. | 3 | 205 |
|  | 5 | 205 |
|  | 10 | 205 |
|  | 14 | 183 |
|  | 22 | 121 |
|  | 34 | 152 |
|  | 35 | 152 |
| xliv. | 1 | 152 |
|  | 23 | 205 |
|  | 26 | 205 |
| xlvi. | 15 | 107 |
| xlvii. | 4 | 118 |
| xlix. | 13 | 65 |
|  | 33 | 28 |
| l. | 25 | 196 |
|  | 26 | 120 |

### EXODUS.

| Chap. | Ver. | Page. |
|---|---|---|
| i. | 7 | 115 |
| iii. | 5 | 79 |
| iv. | 18 | 205 |
| v. | 8 | 20 |
|  | 19 | 20 |
| vi. | 14 | 107 |
| ix. | 16 | 117 |
|  | 24 | 44 |
|  | 31 | 33 |
| x. | 19 | 115 |
|  | 26 | 65 |
| xii. | 9 | 156 |
|  | 16 | 122 |
|  | 33 | 81 |
|  | 45 | 65 |

## INDEX OF TEXTS.

### Exodus—(con.)

| Chap. | Ver. | Page. |
|---|---|---|
| xiii. | 19 | 196 |
|  | 21 | 118 |
| xiv. | 8 | 65 |
|  | 13 | 78 |
|  | 26 | 77 |
| xv. | 18 | 176 |
|  | 26 | 183 |
| xvi. | 4 | 155 |
|  | 16 | 26 |
|  | 27 | 117 |
| xvii. | 7 | 155 |
| xviii. | 4 | 64 |
| xix. | 6 | 65 |
|  | 16 | 39, 115 |
| xx. | 18 | 48 |
| xxi. | 15 | 183 |
|  | 16 | 183 |
|  | 29 | 139 |
|  | 36 | 139 |
| xxii. | 8 | 205 |
| xxiii. | 11 | 73 |
|  | 12 | 73 |
|  | 26 | 160 |
| xxv. | 18 | 98 |
|  | 20 | 98 |
|  | 22 | 57 |
|  | 25 | 65 |
|  | 30 | 138 |
| xxvi. | 14 | 56 |
|  | 17 | 99 |
| xxviii. | 32 | 63 |
| xxix. | 28 | 66 |
|  | 40 | 66 |
| xxx. | 15 | 167 |

### Exodus—(con.)

| Chap. | Ver. | Page. |
|---|---|---|
| xxx. | 23 | 153 |
| xxxii. | 20 | 26 |
| xxxiii. | 4 | 43 |
|  | 15 | 196 |
| xxxv. | 23 | 18, 29 |
|  | 25 | 91 |
|  | 35 | 171, 172 |
| xxxvi. | 19 | 57 |
|  | 22 | 99 |
|  | 29 | 88 |
| xxxvii. | 9 | 98 |
|  | 26 | 91 |
| xl. | 37 | 110 |

### LEVITICUS.

| Chap. | Ver. | Page. |
|---|---|---|
| viii. | 4 | 39 |
| ix. | 17 | 134, 135 |
|  | 22 | 124, 183 |
| x. | 1 | 87, 146 |
|  | 12 | 134, 147 |
|  | 14 | 107 |
| xi. | 1 | 121 |
|  | 31 | 107 |
| xiii. | 1 | 121 |
| xv. | 1 | 121 |
| xvii. | 3 | 101 |
| xx. | 2 | 82 |
|  | 8 | 183 |
|  | 11 | 88 |
|  | 12 | 88 |
|  | 13 | 88 |
|  | 18 | 88 |
| xxiii. | 12 | 63, 67 |

## INDEX OF TEXTS.

| Leviticus—(con.) | | | Numbers—(con.) | | |
|---|---|---|---|---|---|
| Chap. | Ver. | Page. | Chap. | Ver. | Page. |
| xxiii. ... | 22 ... | 168 | xii. ... | 3 ... | 127 |
|  | 38 ... | 135 |  | 14 ... | 78 |
| xxiv. ... | 16 ... | 82 |  | 15 ... | 78 |
|  | 20 ... | 77 |  | 18 ... | 205 |
|  | 23 ... | 83 |  | 19 ... | 205 |
| xxv. ... | 47 ... | 134 |  | 20 ... | 205 |
| xxvi. ... | 34 ... | 153 | xiii. ... | 18 ... | 38 |
|  | 35 ... | 153 |  | 28 ... | 38, 107 |
| xxvii. ... | 16 ... | 67 |  | 31 ... | 106 |
|  | 27 ... | 73 | xiv. ... | 7 ... | 115 |
|  |  |  |  | 10 ... | 83 |
| NUMBERS. | | |  | 13 ... | 179 |
| Chap. | Ver. | Page. | xv. ... | 35 ... | 83 |
| i. ... | 44 ... | 148 |  | 36 ... | 83 |
| ii. ... | 24 ... | 67 | xvi. ... | 3 ... | 39 |
|  | 34 ... | 144 |  | 32 ... | 150 |
| iv. ... | 45 ... | 107 |  | 33 ... | 150 |
| v. ... | 20 ... | 72, 132 |  | 49 ... | 134 |
|  | 26 ... | 66 | xvii. ... | 5 ... | 173 |
| vi. ... | 9 ... | 134 |  | 8 ... | 79 |
| vii. ... | 13 ... | 88 |  | 27 ... | 205 |
|  | 19 ... | 88 |  | 29 ... | 143 |
|  | 25 ... | 88 | xix. ... | 13 ... | 79 |
|  | 31 ... | 88 | xx. ... | 17 ... | 156 |
|  | 37 ... | 88 | xxi. ... | 2 ... | 74 |
|  | 43 ... | 88 |  | 32 ... | 15 |
|  | 49 ... | 88 | xxii. ... | 29 ... | 74 |
|  | 55 ... | 88 | xxiii. ... | 5 ... | 121 |
|  | 61 ... | 88 |  | 10 ... | 95 |
|  | 67 ... | 88 |  | 12 ... | 121 |
|  | 73 ... | 88 |  | 16 ... | 121 |
|  | 79 ... | 88 |  | 19 ... | 101 |
| ix. ... | 16 ... | 138 | xxv. ... | 13 ... | 121 |
|  | 18 ... | 153 | xxviii. ... | 10 ... | 135 |

## INDEX OF TEXTS.

| Numbers—(con.) | | | Deuteronomy—(con.) | | |
|---|---|---|---|---|---|
| Chap. | Ver. | Page. | Chap. | Ver. | Page |
| xxviii. | 15 | 135 | v. | 32 | 156 |
|  | 24 | 135 | vi. | 23 | 196 |
|  | 31 | 135 |  | 24 | 138 |
| xxix. | 6 | 135 | vii. | 4 | 168 |
|  | 11 | 135 | viii. | 2 | 155 |
|  | 16 | 135 |  | 9 | 208 |
|  | 19 | 135 |  | 13 | 44 |
|  | 22 | 135 |  | 14 | 165 |
|  | 25 | 135 |  | 15 | 165 |
|  | 28 | 135 | ix. | 12 | 196 |
|  | 31 | 135 | x. | 5 | 106 |
|  | 34 | 135 |  | 14 | 42 |
|  | 38 | 135 |  | 15 | 128 |
|  | 39 | 135 | xi. | 1 | 138 |
| xxx. | 6 | 63 |  | 12 | 138 |
|  | 14 | 111 |  | 30 | 134 |
|  | 16 | 67, 106 | xii. | 22 | 45 |
| xxxi. | 28 | 89 | xiii. | 9 | 139 |
|  | 30 | 89 |  | 10 | 83 |
| xxxvi. | 5 | 115 | xiv. | 2 | 128 |
|  |  |  |  | 23 | 138 |
| DEUTERONOMY. | | |  | 27 | 159 |
| Chap. | Ver. | Page. |  | 29 | 159 |
| i. | 1 | 106 | xvi. | 21 | 134 |
|  | 11 | 153 | xvii. | 7 | 138 |
|  | 39 | 181 |  | 11 | 156 |
| ii. | 5 | 154 |  | 20 | 156 |
|  | 7 | 72 | xviii. | 1 | 159 |
|  | 24 | 72 |  | 8 | 135 |
|  | 27 | 121 | xix. | 2 | 83 |
| iv. | 1 | 118 |  | 3 | 83 |
|  | 42 | 139 |  | 4 | 139 |
| v. | 15 | 196 |  | 6 | 139 |
|  | 29 | 66, 138 |  | 19 | 8 |

## INDEX OF TEXTS.

| Deuteronomy—(con.) | | |
|---|---|---|
| Chap. | Ver. | Page. |
| xxi. | 1 | 83 |
|  | 21 | 83 |
| xxii. | 1 | 172 |
|  | 2 | 172 |
|  | 21 | 83 |
|  | 22 | 67 |
|  | 24 | 83 |
| xxiii. | 18 | 88 |
| xxiv. | 1 | 121 |
|  | 3 | 121 |
| xxv. | 11 | 118 |
| xxvi. | 3 | 118 |
| xxvii. | 2 | 79 |
|  | 4 | 79, 107 |
|  | 8 | 112 |
| xxviii. | 1 | 128 |
|  | 14 | 156 |
|  | 29 | 138 |
| xxix. | 5 | 168 |
|  | 10 | 86 |
|  | 11 | 168 |
| xxxi. | 6 | 156 |
|  | 27 | 141 |
| xxxii. | 29 | 95 |
|  | 30 | 205 |
| xxxiii. | 17 | 88 |
|  | 29 | 73 |
| xxxiv. | 4 | 80 |

### JOSHUA.

| Chap. | Ver. | Page. |
|---|---|---|
| i. | 6 | 156, 157 |
|  | 7 | 156, 157 |
|  | 11 | 83 |

| Joshua—(con.) | | |
|---|---|---|
| Chap. | Ver. | Page. |
| ii. | 2 | 118 |
| v. | 15 | 79 |
| vi. | 21 | 90 |
| vii. | 9 | 178 |
|  | 12 | 205 |
|  | 25 | 83 |
| ix. | 8 | 196 |
| x. | 18 | 118 |
| xii. | 9 | 134 |
| xvi. | 10 | 15 |
| xvii. | 18 | 183 |
| xxi. | 42 | 144 |
| xxii. | 14 | 144 |
| xxiii. | 6 | 156 |
| xxiv. | 13 | 166 |

### JUDGES.

| Chap. | Ver. | Page. |
|---|---|---|
| i. | 20 | 15 |
|  | 21 | 185 |
| ii. | 22 | 155 |
| iii. | 17 | 54 |
| iv. | 21 | 66, 67 |
| vi. | 13 | 110, 202 |
|  | 15 | 202 |
|  | 31 | 110 |
| vii. | 10 | 120 |
|  | 14 | 91 |
| viii. | 5 | 106 |
|  | 18 | 148 |
| ix. | 33 | 37 |
|  | 34 | 37 |
| xi. | 26 | 107 |
| xii. | 6 | 113 |

# INDEX OF TEXTS.

| Judges—(con.) | | |
|---|---|---|
| Chap. | Ver. | Page. |
| xiii. | 4 | 179 |
|  | 7 | 159 |
| xiv. | 16 | 156 |
| xx. | 16 | 66 |
|  | 48 | 88 |

## RUTH.

| Chap. | Ver. | Page. |
|---|---|---|
| i. | 18 | 117 |
| ii. | 14 | 134 |
| iv. | 1 | 70 |
|  | 7 | 118 |
|  | 11 | 72 |
|  | 12 | 72 |

## 1 SAMUEL.

| Chap. | Ver. | Page. |
|---|---|---|
| i. | 6 | 118 |
|  | 13 | 83 |
| ii. | 2 | 135 |
|  | 29 | 27 |
|  | 34 | 88 |
| vi. | 12 | 156 |
| ix. | 22 | 27 |
| x. | 5 | 67 |
| xii. | 8 | 165 |
| xiv. | 7 | 72 |
| xv. | 3 | 90 |
| xvii. | 5 | 66 |
|  | 38 | 66 |
| xix. | 11 | 180, 181 |
| xx. | 14 | 141 |
|  | 20 | 205 |
| xxi. | 7 | 27 |

| 1 Samuel—(con.) | | |
|---|---|---|
| Chap. | Ver. | Page. |
| xxi. | 9 | 131 |
| xxiv. | 11 | 73 |
| xxv. | 22 | 153 |
|  | 34 | 205 |
| xxix. | 6 | 41 |
|  | 8 | 153 |
| xxx. | 6 | 82 |

## 2 SAMUEL.

| Chap. | Ver. | Page. |
|---|---|---|
| i. | 4 | 106 |
|  | 5 | 106 |
|  | 25 | 64 |
| ii. | 19 | 156 |
| iii. | 13 | 205 |
|  | 17 | 139 |
| iv. | 6 | 205 |
|  | 8 | 123 |
| v. | 2 | 140 |
|  | 6 | 205 |
| vii. | 22 | 135 |
|  | 23 | 169 |
|  | 28 | 107 |
| viii. | 1 | 209 |
| ix. | 10 | 138 |
| x. | 4 | 148 |
| xi. | 8 | 72 |
|  | 10 | 72 |
| xii. | 2 | 116 |
|  | 18 | 141 |
|  | 21 | 141 |
|  | 22 | 141 |
|  | 33 | 116 |
| xiv. | 5 | 73, 81 |

## INDEX OF TEXTS.

### 2 Samuel—(con.)

| Chap. | Ver. | Page. |
|---|---|---|
| xiv. | 6 | 72 |
|  | 7 | 72 |
|  | 15 | 72 |
|  | 17 | 72 |
| xv. | 30 | 39 |
| xviii. | 25 | 43 |
| xxi. | 16 | 10 |
| xxiii. | 1 | 107 |

### 1 KINGS.

| Chap. | Ver. | Page. |
|---|---|---|
| i. | 14 | 141 |
| ii. | 23 | 108 |
|  | 26 | 186 |
| iii. | 16 | 52 |
| iv. | 30 | 126 |
|  | 31 | 126 |
| vi. | 23 | 98 |
|  | 24 | 184 |
|  | 27 | 98 |
| vii. | 31 | 66 |
| viii. | 1 | 79 |
|  | 5 | 24 |
|  | 6 | 122 |
|  | 42 | 181 |
|  | 54 | 79 |
| ix. | 15 | 118 |
| x. | 7 | 35 |
|  | 15 | 40 |
|  | 19 | 145 |
|  | 21 | 71, 183 |
|  | 24 | 121 |
| xi. | 26 | 81 |
| xii. | 18 | 83 |

### 1 Kings—(con.)

| Chap. | Ver. | Page. |
|---|---|---|
| xii. | 27 | 181 |
| xiii. | 6 | 77 |
|  | 14 | 184 |
|  | 26 | 165 |
| xv. | 22 | 183 |
| xvii. | 9 | 81 |
|  | 14 | 108 |
| xviii. | 3 | 165 |
|  | 12 | 181 |
|  | 14 | 181 |
|  | 21 | 110 |
| xix. | 19 | 165 |
| xx. | 3 | 41 |
|  | 20 | 66 |
| xxi. | 13 | 83 |

### 2 KINGS.

| Chap. | Ver. | Page. |
|---|---|---|
| i. | 8 | 27, 68 |
| ii. | 10 | 68 |
|  | 11 | 68, 85 |
|  | 19 | 16 |
| iii. | 16 | 200 |
|  | 17 | 200 |
| iv. | 1 | 73 |
|  | 24 | 205 |
|  | 39 | 117 |
| vi. | 15 | 66 |
| vii. | 2 | 80 |
| ix. | 30 | 22 |
| x. | 15 | 72 |
| xi. | 2 | 200 |
|  | 21 | 200 |

## INDEX OF TEXTS.

| 2 Kings—(con.) | | |
|---|---|---|
| Chap. | Ver. | Page. |
| xii. | 1 | 200 |
|  | 2 | 200 |
|  | 4 | 200 |
|  | 6 | 200 |
|  | 7 | 200 |
|  | 11 | 24 |
|  | 18 | 200 |
|  | 19 | 200 |
|  | 20 | 200 |
| xiii. | 1 | 200 |
|  | 9 | 200 |
|  | 10 | 200 |
|  | 12 | 200 |
|  | 13 | 200 |
|  | 14 | 200 |
|  | 25 | 200 |
| xiv. | 1 | 200 |
|  | 8 | 99 |
|  | 11 | 99 |
|  | 13 | 200 |
| xv. | 19 | 118 |
| xvi. | 8 | 44 |
| xviii. | 18 | 165 |
|  | 34 | 43 |
|  | 37 | 165 |
| xix. | 13 | 42 |
|  | 28 | 208 |
|  | 35 | 212 |
| xx. | 3 | 15 |
|  | 4 | 15 |
| xxii. | 2 | 156 |
| xxiii. | 29 | 163 |
| xxv. | 5 | 50 |
|  | 10 | 51 |

| 1 CHRONICLES. | | |
|---|---|---|
| Chap. | Ver. | Page. |
| vii. | 3 | 88 |
| ix. | 20 | 139 |
| xi. | 2 | 140 |
| xiii. | 6 | 195 |
| xvi. | 36 | 176 |
| xvii. | 16 | 63 |
| xix. | 3 | 118 |
| xxi. | 3 | 153 |
| xxii. | 5 | 116 |
| xxiii. | 17 | 131 |
| xxviii. | 2 | 79 |
| xxix. | 7 | 67 |
|  | 10 | 176 |
|  | 11 | 42 |

| 2 CHRONICLES. | | |
|---|---|---|
| Chap. | Ver. | Page. |
| i. | 12 | 34 |
| ii. | 9 | 116 |
| v. | 12 | 88 |
| vi. | 14 | 159, 165 |
|  | 15 | 165 |
|  | 18 | 15 |
|  | 33 | 15 |
| vii. | 22 | 165 |
| viii. | 18 | 195 |
| ix. | 8 | 118 |
|  | 11 | 71 |
|  | 18 | 145 |
|  | 23 | 120 |
| x. | 16 | 144 |
|  | 18 | 83 |
| xi. | 18 | 128 |

## INDEX OF TEXTS.

### 2 Chronicles—(con.)

| Chap. | Ver. | Page. |
|---|---|---|
| xi. | 20 | 128 |
|  | 21 | 128 |
| xv. | 2 | 141 |
| xvi. | 1 | 157 |
| xvii. | 19 | 135 |
|  | 6 | 135 |
| xviii. | 9 | 144,145,146 |
| xxiv. | 21 | 83 |
| xxv. | 17 | 99 |
|  | 19 | 64 |
|  | 21 | 99 |
| xxviii. | 6 | 53 |
| xxix. | 8 | 66 |
| xxxii. | 7 | 39, 40 |
| xxxiv. | 3 | 141 |
|  | 4 | 26 |

### EZRA.

| Chap. | Ver. | Page. |
|---|---|---|
| vii. | 27 | 121 |
| viii. | 20 | 88 |
|  | 22 | 41 |
|  | 33 | 41, 45 |
| ix. | 7 | 116 |

### NEHEMIAH.

| Chap. | Ver. | Page. |
|---|---|---|
| ii. | 2 | 91 |
|  | 5 | 110 |
|  | 10 | 119 |
|  | 12 | 121 |
| iii. | 23 | 133 |
| iv. | 3 | 181 |
| vii. | 5 | 63, 121 |

### Nehemiah—(con.)

| Chap. | Ver. | Page. |
|---|---|---|
| ix. | 5 | 176 |
|  | 19 | 117 |
| xii. | 27 | 90 |

### ESTHER.

| Chap. | Ver. | Page. |
|---|---|---|
| i. | 17 | 181 |
|  | 20 | 181 |
| ii. | 11 | 181 |
|  | 14 | 205 |
|  | 17 | 127 |
| iii. | 8 | 128 |
| iv. | 4 | 116 |
|  | 14 | 110 |
| v. | 3 | 204 |
|  | 7 |  |
|  | 13 | 153 |
| vi. | 13 | 110 |
| viii. | 5 | 110 |

### JOB.

| Chap. | Ver. | Page. |
|---|---|---|
| i. | 7 | 196 |
|  | 10 | 66 |
| ii. | 2 | 196 |
| iii. | 16 | 66 |
|  | 17 | 107 |
|  | 18 | 107 |
| v. | 9 | 165 |
|  | 11 | 107 |
| vii. | 9 | 84 |
|  | 16 | 138 |
|  | 19 | 149 |
| viii. | 7 | 95 |

## INDEX OF TEXTS.

### Job—(con.)

| Chap. | Ver. | Page. |
|---|---|---|
| viii. | 20 | 60 |
| ix. | 30 | 161 |
| x. | 18 | 70 |
|  | 19 | 205 |
| xii. | 2 | 85 |
|  | 13 | 36 |
|  | 16 | 41 |
| xiv. | 3 | 70 |
| xv. | 21 | 46 |
| xviii. | 2 | 139 |
| xix. | 3 | 25 |
| xx. | 15 | 78, 149 |
|  | 18 | 149 |
|  | 23 | 141 |
| xxi. | 21 | 46 |
| xxiv. | 15 | 70 |
|  | 25 | 109 |
| xxv. | 6 | 100 |
| xxvii. | 6 | 153 |
| xxviii. | 22 | 80 |
| xxx. | 1 | 9 |
|  | 5 | 55 |
| xxxi. | 11 | 66 |
| xxxiv. | 33 | 204 |
| xxxv. | 8 | 100, 101 |
| xxxvi. | 20 | 39 |
| xxxix. | 16 | 205 |
|  | 25 | 209 |
| xl. | 8 | 31 |
| xlii. | 12 | 95 |

### PSALMS.

| Chap. | Ver. | Page. |
|---|---|---|
| vii. | 2 | 141 |

### Psalms—(con.)

| Chap. | Ver. | Page. |
|---|---|---|
| vii. | 9 | 203 |
|  | 10 | 165 |
| viii. | 4 | 101 |
| ix. | 5 | 175 |
| x. | 16 | 176 |
| xiv. | 2 | 204 |
| xvi. | 8 | 138 |
| xvii. | 7 | 60 |
| xix. | 11 | 124 |
| xxi. | 4 | 176 |
| xxiii. | 6 | 181 |
| xxv. | 16 | 170 |
|  | 17 | 202 |
|  | 20 | 202 |
| xxvii. | 7 | 80 |
|  | 13 | 206 |
| xxxiii. | 19 | 118 |
| xxxiv. | 18 | 105 |
| xxxv. | 14 | 205 |
|  | 26 | 64 |
| xxxvi. | 10 | 202 |
| xxxviii. | 4 | 66 |
| xl. | 3 | 121 |
|  | 12 | 73 |
| xliii. | 1 | 202 |
|  | 3 | 202 |
| xliv. | 26 | 84 |
| xlv. | 6 | 176 |
|  | 17 | 176 |
| xlviii. | 14 | 176 |
| xlix. | 7 | 160 |
|  | 18 | 141 |
| l. | 21 | 70 |
| lii. | 8 | 176 |

## INDEX OF TEXTS.

| Psalms—(con.) | | | Psalms—(con.) | | |
|---|---|---|---|---|---|
| Chap. | Ver. | Page. | Chap. | Ver. | Page. |
| liv. | 4 | 64 | xcviii. | 1 | 45 |
| lvi. | 8 | 24 | c. | 3 | 210 |
| lviii. | 5 | 161 | ci. | 2 | 202 |
|  | 7 | 205 | cii. | 27 | 70 |
| lxi. | 7 | 202 | ciii. | 5 | 209 |
| lxii. | 7 | 41 |  | 9 | 138 |
| lxiii. | 4 | 141 |  | 10 | 157 |
| lxiv. | 6 | 41 | civ. | 1 | 19 |
| lxvii. | 4 | 202 |  | 33 | 141 |
| lxviii. | 21 | 70 | cvi. | 4 | 202 |
| lxix. | 6 | 172 | cix. | 26 | 202 |
|  | 16 | 170 | cxix. | 8 | 202 |
|  | 31 | 101 |  | 10 | 202 |
| lxxi. | 8 | 74 |  | 44 | 176 |
| lxxii. | 5 | 152 |  | 50 | 73 |
| lxxiii. | 26 | 43, 44 |  | 92 | 73, 206 |
| lxxiv. | 19 | 202 |  | 96 | 116 |
|  | 21 | 202 |  | 97 | 202 |
| lxxx. | 17 | 100 |  | 112 | 73 |
| lxxxiv. | 2 | 44 |  | 147 | 21 |
|  | 10 | 190 |  | 161 | 73 |
| lxxxv. | 12 | 181 | cxxiv. | 8 | 165 |
|  | 13 | 181 | cxxv. | 4 | 105 |
| lxxxvi. | 16 | 202 | cxxvii. | 1 | 205 |
| lxxxvii. | 5 | 45 | cxxxi. | 1 | 183 |
| lxxxviii. | 10 | 18 | cxxxii. | 4 | 157 |
|  | 13 | 21 | cxxxv. | 21 | 165 |
| lxxxix. | 47 | 202 | cxxxix. | 4 | 61 |
| xc. | 14 | 202 |  | 10 | 181 |
| xciii. | 1 | 18, 19 |  | 24 | 204 |
|  | 2 | 19 | cxliv. | 3 | 101 |
| xciv. | 17 | 206 |  | 14 | 41 |
| xcv. | 6 | 201 | cxlv. | 1 | 176 |
|  | 7 | 201, 210 |  | 2 | 176 |

## INDEX OF TEXTS.

### Psalms—(con.)

| Chap. | Ver. | Page. |
|---|---|---|
| cxlvi. ... | 3 ... | 100 |
|  | 5 ... | 166 |
|  | 6 ... | 166 |
|  | 7 ... | 166 |
| cxlvii. ... | 4 ... | 24 |
|  | 7 ... | 166 |
|  | 8 ... | 166 |
|  | 11 ... | 171 |
|  | 20 ... | 128 |
| cxlviii. ... | 6 ... | 176 |

### PROVERBS.

| Chap. | Ver. | Page. |
|---|---|---|
| i. ... | 16 ... | 118 |
|  | 23 ... | 170 |
|  | 27 ... | 34, 43 |
| ii. ... | 6 ... | 43 |
| iii. ... | 16 ... | 187 |
| iv. ... | 16 ... | 206 |
|  | 27 ... | 156 |
| v. ... | 11 ... | 44 |
|  | 19 ... | 138 |
| vi. ... | 16 ... | 104 |
| viii. ... | 30 ... | 138 |
| x. ... | 22 ... | 93 |
|  | 24 ... | 94 |
| xvi. ... | 18 ... | 66 |
|  | 24 ... | 66 |
| xvii. ... | 15 ... | 87 |
| xviii. ... | 4 ... | 188 |
|  | 11 ... | 67 |
| xix. ... | 2 ... | 94 |
| xx. ... | 3 ... | 74 |

### Proverbs—(con.)

| Chap. | Ver. | Page. |
|---|---|---|
| xx. ... | 10 ... | 88 |
|  | 12 ... | 88 |
|  | 14 ... | 16 |
|  | 17 ... | 139 |
| xxi. ... | 8 ... | 116 |
|  | 20 ... | 42, 149 |
| xxiv. ... | 10 ... | 110 |
|  | 21 ... | 171 |
| xxv. ... | 16 ... | 153 |
|  | 20 ... | 207 |
| xxvi. ... | 4 ... | 92 |
| xxvii. ... | 3 ... | 212 |
|  | 9 ... | 50 |
| xxviii. ... | 8 ... | 19 |
|  | 14 ... | 138 |
| xxix. ... | 12 ... | 107 |
| xxx. ... | 2 ... | 129 |
|  | 13 ... | 202 |
|  | 18 ... | 104 |
|  | 24 ... | 104, 116 |
|  | 29 ... | 104 |
| xxxi. ... | 26 ... | 60 |

### ECCLESIASTES.

| Chap. | Ver. | Page. |
|---|---|---|
| ii. ... | 13 ... | 153 |
| iii. ... | 12 ... | 153 |
| iv. ... | 8 ... | 70 |
|  | 16 ... | 70 |
| v. ... | 2 ... | 55, 188 |
|  | 8 ... | 27 |
| vii. ... | 24 ... | 116 |
| ix. ... | 8 ... | 138 |
| xii. ... | 12 ... | 70 |

## CANTICLES.

| Chap. | Ver. | Page. |
|---|---|---|
| ii. | 5 | 212 |
| v. | 8 | 212 |
|  | 10 | 27 |
| vii. | 12 | 204 |

## ISAIAH.

| Chap. | Ver. | Page. |
|---|---|---|
| i. | 6 | 28 |
|  | 9 | 205 |
| iii. | 7 | 66 |
| v. | 7 | 189 |
|  | 10 | 26 |
|  | 13 | 39 |
|  | 29 | 209 |
| vi. | 2 | 148 |
| vii. | 19 | 88 |
| viii. | 6 | 37 |
| ix. | 7 | 70 |
|  | 13 | 38 |
| xi. | 9 | 156 |
|  | 11 | 211 |
| xiv. | 27 | 31 |
| xvi. | 11 | 66 |
| xxii. | 16 | 66 |
| xxiii. | 16 | 67 |
| xxv. | 4 | 184 |
| xxviii. | 18 | 31 |
|  | 29 | 165 |
| xxix. | 8 | 66 |
| xxx. | 8 | 176 |
|  | 13 | 67 |
|  | 17 | 66 |
|  | 28 | 209 |

## Isaiah—(con.)

| Chap. | Ver. | Page. |
|---|---|---|
| xxxi. | 6 | 170 |
| xxxii. | 2 | 66 |
|  | 4 | 113 |
| xxxiv. | 10 | 156, 176 |
|  | 16 | 71, 92 |
| xxxv. | 6 | 66 |
|  | 8 | 201 |
| xxxvi. | 19 | 43 |
| xxxvii. | 29 | 208 |
|  | 36 | 212 |
| xli. | 22 | 117 |
| xliii. | 11 | 135 |
|  | 13 | 23 |
| xliv. | 6 | 135 |
|  | 8 | 135 |
| xlv. | 6 | 135 |
|  | 24 | 45 |
| xlvii. | 9 | 123 |
|  | 10 | 34 |
|  | 13 | 17 |
| xlviii. | 5 | 45, 92 |
| xlix. | 22 | 73 |
|  | 26 | 54 |
|  | 5 | 28 |
| l. | 6 | 28 |
| li. | 6 | 84 |
|  | 8 | 148 |
|  | 12 | 101 |
|  | 23 | 121 |
| lii. | 14 | 15 |
| liii. | 2 | 159 |
| lv. | 6 | 141 |
|  | 10 | 47 |
| lvi. | 2 | 101 |

# INDEX OF TEXTS. xxxvii.

## Isaiah—(con.)

| Chap. | Ver. | Page. |
|---|---|---|
| lvi. | 7 | 73 |
| lvii. | 2 | 148 |
|  | 16 | 138, 181 |
| lix. | 21 | 58, 121 |
| lx. | 11 | 156 |
|  | 17 | 73 |
| lxi. | 1 | 17 |
| lxiii. | 11 | 211 |
|  | 15 | 42 |
| lxv. | 25 | 156 |

## JEREMIAH.

| Chap. | Ver. | Page. |
|---|---|---|
| ii. | 10 | 204 |
| iv. | 22 | 37 |
| v. | 1 | 204 |
|  | 9 | 123 |
|  | 23 | 37 |
|  | 29 | 123 |
| vi. | 7 | 42, 45 |
|  | 20 | 50 |
| vii. | 7 | 176 |
|  | 16 | 37 |
| viii. | 5 | 37 |
| ix. | 9 | 123 |
| xi. | 8 | 144 |
|  | 19 | 80 |
| xii. | 4 | 95 |
| xiv. | 9 | 16 |
|  | 11 | 37 |
|  | 18 | 212 |
| xv. | 9 | 141 |
| xvi. | 12 | 144 |

## Jeremiah—(con.)

| Chap. | Ver. | Page. |
|---|---|---|
| xvi. | 16 | 138 |
| xvii. | 9 | 129 |
| xviii. | 9 | 118 |
|  | 15 | 37 |
|  | 18 | 80 |
| xxii. | 17 | 118 |
| xxiii. | 14 | 66 |
|  | 29 | 67 |
| xxv. | 5 | 176 |
| xxvi. | 15 | 181 |
| xxx. | 2 | 56 |
| xxxi. | 32 | 210 |
| xxxiii. | 13 | 24 |
| xxxiv. | 9 | 71 |
|  | 10 | 71 |
|  | 11 | 138, 139 |
| xxxvii. | 4 | 121 |
|  | 15 | 121 |
|  | 18 | 121 |
| xxxviii. | 7 | 69 |
| xl. | 4 | 117 |
|  | 5 | 141 |
| xlii. | 18 | 47 |
| xliv. | 6 | 47 |
| xlvi. | 12 | 87 |
| xlviii. | 33 | 45 |
| xlix. | 6 | 138 |
|  | 9 | 17 |
|  | 18 | 101 |
|  | 24 | 45 |
|  | 33 | 101 |
| l. | 6 | 37 |
|  | 40 | 101 |
| li. | 43 | 101 |

## LAMENTATIONS.

| Chap. | Ver. | Page. |
|---|---|---|
| i. | 9 | 95 |
|  | 12 | 204 |
| ii. | 12 | 42 |
|  | 19 | 72 |
| iii. | 38 | 50 |
|  | 47 | 34 |

## EZEKIEL.

| Chap. | Ver. | Page. |
|---|---|---|
| i. | 11 | 98 |
| ii. | 10 | 42 |
| iii. | 5 | 66, 68 |
|  | 6 | 66, 68 |
|  | 15 | 16 |
| iv. | 4 | 99 |
|  | 8 | 99 |
| vii. | 2 | 97 |
|  | 15 | 189 |
|  | 16 | 88 |
| xiii. | 11 | 214 |
|  | 15 | 214 |
| xiv. | 16 | 180 |
|  | 18 | 180 |
|  | 20 | 180 |
| xvi. | 5 | 70 |
|  | 13 | 116 |
|  | 40 | 83 |
| xx. | 8 | 144 |
|  | 40 | 88 |
| xxi. | 29 | 141 |
| xxii. | 6 | 143 |
| xxix. | 21 | 67 |
| xxxi. | 4 | 30 |
|  | 17 | 105 |

## Ezekiel—(con.)

| Chap. | Ver. | Page. |
|---|---|---|
| xxxi. | 18 | 105 |
| xxxii. | 25 | 105 |
|  | 30 | 105 |
| xxxiii. | 11 | 170 |
|  | 20 | 143 |
| xxxvii. | 16 | 99 |
|  | 17 | 99 |
| xxxix. | 12 | 124 |
| xlii. | 13 | 105 |
| xliii. | 1 | 138 |
|  | 19 | 106 |
| xliv. | 8 | 73 |
|  | 13 | 73 |
|  | 17 | 141 |
| xlv. | 11 | 26, 67 |

## DANIEL.

| Chap. | Ver. | Page. |
|---|---|---|
| ii. | 10 | 159 |
|  | 11 | 131, 206 |
|  | 20 | 176 |
| iii. | 22 | 116 |
|  | 28 | 206 |
| iv. | 10 | 64 |
|  | 14 | 173 |
|  | 15 | 173 |
|  | 19 | 16, 157 |
|  | 21 | 189 |
|  | 23 | 67 |
|  | 31 | 141 |
| v. | 6 | 97 |
|  | 11 | 35 |
|  | 14 | 35 |
| vi. | 5 | 205 |

# INDEX OF TEXTS.

### Daniel—(con.)

| Chap. | Ver. | Page. |
|---|---|---|
| vi. ... | 10 ... | 79 |
| | 11 ... | 80 |
| | 15 ... | 159 |
| | 23 ... | 116 |
| vii. ... | 11 ... | 80 |
| | 14 ... | 45 |
| | 15 ... | 81 |
| | 18 ... | 176 |
| | 19 ... | 116 |
| viii. ... | 5 ... | 67 |
| | 13 ... | 67 |
| | 27 ... | 16 |
| ix. ... | 17 ... | 54 |
| | 20 ... | 141 |
| | 21 ... | 141 |
| x. ... | 5 ... | 189 |
| | 6 ... | 189 |
| | 21 ... | 142 |
| xi. ... | 25 ... | 80 |
| xii. ... | 3 ... | 176 |

### HOSEA.

| Chap. | Ver. | Page. |
|---|---|---|
| vi. ... | 11 ... | 67 |
| vii. ... | 6 ... | 141 |

### JOEL.

| Chap. | Ver. | Page. |
|---|---|---|
| i. ... | 13 ... | 42 |
| ii. ... | 6 ... | 28 |
| | 14 ... | 204 |
| iii. ... | 3 ... | 63 |

### AMOS.

| Chap. | Ver. | Page. |
|---|---|---|
| iii. ... | 3 ... | 205 |
| vi. ... | 2 ... | 104 |
| vii. ... | 14 ... | 67 |
| ix. ... | 1 ... | 88 |
| | 2 ... | 195 |
| | 3 ... | 195 |
| | 4 ... | 195 |

### OBADIAH.

| Chap. | Ver. | Page. |
|---|---|---|
| i. ... | 3 ... | 191 |
| | 4 ... | 190, 194 |
| | 16 ... | 205 |

### JONAH.

| Chap. | Ver. | Page. |
|---|---|---|
| i. ... | 10 ... | 116 |
| iii. ... | 8 ... | 143 |
| | 9 ... | 205 |

### MICAH.

| Chap. | Ver. | Page. |
|---|---|---|
| i. ... | 11 ... | 170 |
| iv. ... | 3 ... | 17 |
| | 5 ... | 176 |
| | 13 ... | 72 |
| v. ... | 7 ... | 47 |
| vii. ... | 1 ... | 17 |

### NAHUM.

| Chap. | Ver. | Page. |
|---|---|---|
| ii. ... | 9 ... | 70 |
| | 10 ... | 28 |

## INDEX OF TEXTS.

### Nahum—(con.)
| Chap. | Ver. | Page. |
|---|---|---|
| iii. | 3 | 70 |
| | 15 | 17 |

### HABAKKUK.
| Chap. | Ver. | Page. |
|---|---|---|
| iii. | 10 | 30 |

### ZEPHANIAH.
| Chap. | Ver. | Page. |
|---|---|---|
| i. | 10 | 67 |
| ii. | 5 | 71 |
| iii. | 6 | 71 |

### HAGGAI.
| Chap. | Ver. | Page. |
|---|---|---|
| ii. | 16 | 118 |
| | 19 | 45 |

### ZECHARIAH.
| Chap. | Ver. | Page. |
|---|---|---|
| i. | 19 | 106 |
| iv. | 4 | 106 |
| | 5 | 106 |
| | 11 | 106 |
| | 12 | 106 |
| vii. | 10 | 167 |
| viii. | 17 | 167 |
| ix. | 3 | 17 |
| | 12 | 170 |
| x. | 6 | 205 |
| | 11 | 85 |
| xiii. | 4 | 27, 68 |

### MALACHI.
| Chap. | Ver. | Page. |
|---|---|---|
| i. | 13 | 142 |
| | 14 | 142 |
| iii. | 10 | 17, 204 |

### MATTHEW.
| Chap. | Ver. | Page. |
|---|---|---|
| xvi. | 13 | 100 |
| xviii. | 10 | 49 |

### MARK.
| Chap. | Ver. | Page. |
|---|---|---|
| vii. | 35 | 113 |

### ACTS.
| Chap. | Ver. | Page. |
|---|---|---|
| viii. | 27 | 69 |

### ROMANS.
| Chap. | Ver. | Page. |
|---|---|---|
| i. | 22 | 141 |
| iv. | 3 | 142 |
| xiii. | 7 | 74 |

### 1 CORINTHIANS.
| Chap. | Ver. | Page. |
|---|---|---|
| iv. | 6 | 140 |
| xiv. | 8 | 27 |

### REVELATION.
| Chap. | Ver. | Page. |
|---|---|---|
| xx. | 13 | 30 |

# ECCLESIASTICAL ENGLISH.

## CHAPTER I.

### INTRODUCTORY.

CONTENTS.—Bishop Lowth on the neglect of the study of English. Convocation's vote of thanks to the Revisers. The *Times'* sarcasm on the wording of the vote. Its grammatical errors. Singular and plural mixed. "Expended". Past infinitive for present. Inconsistency the chief characteristic of the Revisers' work. "Which" for "who". Tautology, "the weight in weight".

It is sad to relate that there is nothing new in the fact that Englishmen are often ignorant of English. A century ago it was said, "Is it not amazing that some, who have beyond doubt been very excellent Greek and Latin scholars, have written their mother tongue not only inelegantly, but even very ungrammatically?"—*Baker's Remarks on the English Language, Edition* 1799, *p.* 84.

Bishop Lowth, writing still earlier in the

last century, points out the source of this deficiency. He says, "A grammatical study of our own language makes no part of the ordinary method of instruction which we pass through in our childhood; and it is very seldom that we apply ourselves to it afterward. Yet the want of it will not be effectually supplied by any other advantages whatsoever. Much practice in the polite world, and a general acquaintance with the best authors, are good helps; but alone will hardly be sufficient: we have writers who have enjoyed these advantages in their full extent, and yet cannot be recommended as models of an accurate style. Much less then will what is commonly called Learning serve the purpose; that is, a critical knowledge of ancient languages, and much reading of ancient authors. The greatest critic and most able grammarian of the last age, when he came to apply his learning and his criticisms to an English author, was frequently at a loss in matters of ordinary use and common construction of his own vernacular idiom."—*Preface to*

'*A Short Introduction to English Grammar*', by Dr. Lowth, 1762.

More than one hundred and twenty years have passed since the foregoing was written, yet the lament over the neglect of the study of our language is as applicable to the present generation, as it was to the generation of our forefathers who lived in the days of Bishop Lowth.

This neglect must not be allowed to continue; but how is its continuance to be prevented? I know of no plan so likely to be effectual, as the public exposure of the errors of those persons whose innate delicacy of feeling will render them ashamed of their shortcomings, while their philanthropy will arouse in them the resolve that their influence shall thenceforth be exerted to secure, to the rising generation, freedom from the disgrace of having to blush for their ignorance of the laws governing their own language.

In a former work[*] I exposed the errors and

[*] 'The Revisers' English.'

inconsistencies found in the language of the Revised Version of the *New* Testament. I purpose now to expose the errors and inconsistencies found in the language of the Revised Version of the *Old* Testament, and shall show that they are as gross, as flagrant, and as numerous as are those in the *New*.

But the Revisers are not the only transgressors of the laws of our language. In the resolution which was passed by Convocation to thank the Revisers for their labours, there are errors which would disgrace a school-boy. Yet I have no doubt that the Members of Convocation are, to the present day, in happy ignorance of that fact, and if they chanced to read in our leading daily journal, as they might have done, that their resolution was "*carefully and wisely worded*", they happily failed to see the covert sarcasm of the remark, and smiled complacently at what they in their simplicity believed to be a well-deserved compliment!

It is a pity to awaken them from their dream of self-congratulation; for has it not been said, and is it not generally believed, that

> "Where ignorance is bliss,
> 'Tis folly to be wise."

Still, for the good of others, the dream, however pleasant, must be broken.

The resolution (quoted in *The Times* of May 16th, 1885, p. 11, last column) was as follows:—

> "That this House presents its hearty thanks to the learned Revisers of the Authorised Version of the Old Testament for the unwearied labour and singular diligence which they have expended during many years in carrying out the weighty task intrusted to them by Convocation. They desire to express their great gratitude to Almighty God for permitting so important a work to have been executed at this time, and they pray that it may be blessed by Him to the increase of the knowledge of His Holy Word by His people."

It will be observed that, in the first sentence

of this paragraph, the Members of Convocation speak of themselves collectively, and therefore with strict propriety they employ the singular number and say,

"*This House presents its* hearty thanks to the learned Revisers".

This form, having been adopted at the beginning of the paragraph, should have been continued throughout, and not have been changed into the plural, as it has been in the second sentence, where we read,

"*They* desire to express *their* great gratitude".

The change is the more objectionable because it is momentarily misleading, seeing that the pronoun "*they*", which really refers to the Members of Convocation, does of course grammatically refer to the plural pronoun just preceding it, namely "*them*", i.e., to the "*Revisers*", and not to "*Convocation*", because that term, being used collectively, as I have already remarked, is in the singular number.

The first sentence of the paragraph, then, should have been continued thus :—

"*This House presents its* hearty thanks . . . . . and desires to express *its* great gratitude ".

A second error in the sentence consists in employing the word "*expended*" to describe the rendering of the services of the Revisers. To "*expend*" means to weigh out, the word being derived from the Latin "*ex*", out, and "*pendo*", to weigh; and it implies a certain carefulness of bestowal which is not applicable to the generous manner in which those services were given. But even had it been applicable, its use there could not be designated felicitous, seeing that the word "*weighty*" almost immediately follows it.

But that is not all, another error occurs in the concluding sentence of this short paragraph, viz., the using of the present participle and past infinitive, instead of the past participle and present infinitive. The passage reads thus :—

> "They desire to express their great gratitude to Almighty God for *permitting* so important a work to *have been* executed at this time",

which is equivalent to saying,

> "They desire to express their great gratitude to Almighty God for [*now*] *permitting* so important a work to *have been* executed [*in the past*] at this time"!

They should have said,

> "for *having permitted* so important a work *to be* executed at this time,"

or, better still,

> "for having permitted the accomplishment of so important a work."

That the Revisers themselves would probably have avoided this error, might be inferred from their having corrected a similar one in Deut. xix. 19, where, in the Authorised Version, we read,

> "Then shall ye do unto him as he had thought *to have done* unto his brother."

In the Revised Version it is,

> "Then shall ye do unto him, as he had thought *to do* unto his brother."

Again, in Job xxx. 1, a similar error has been corrected by the Revisers. In the Authorised Version we read,

> "But now they that are younger than I have me in derision, whose fathers I would have disdained *to have set* with the dogs of my flock."

In the Revised Version it is,

> "Whose fathers I disdained *to set* with the dogs of my flock."

Had the Revisers shown the same grammatical acumen throughout their work, as they have shown in these instances, there would have been no necessity for these criticisms. But, unfortunately, *the chief characteristic of the Revisers' work is its inconsistency.* Oftentimes the very error which the Revisers correct in one place, they themselves fall into in another; and not infrequently they render ungrammatical a construction which, if left unaltered, would have remained correct.

Turn now to 2 Sam. xxi. 16, and there you will find a perpetuation of the error which the Revisers had corrected in Deuteronomy and Job. The passage is,

> "He being girded with a new sword, thought *to have slain* David."

But surely what he "*thought*" was not "*to have slain* David", but *to slay* him.

I remark, in passing, that there are four errors in that one verse. It reads as follows,

> "And Ishbi-benob, which [*who*] was of the sons of the giant, the weight of whose spear was three hundred shekels of brass in weight, [the *weight* of it was so much *in weight!*] he [this pronoun is redundant, Ishbi-benob being the nominative to the verb] being girded with a new sword, thought to have slain [*to slay*] David."

As the *Edinburgh Review* of October, 1885, p. 476, remarked, "There is something ludicrously self-contradictory in a Revised Version which revises itself without yet being revised; which was intended to make everything clear, and only makes it clear that what is most important is quite dark."

That the Revisers knew what was required of them is evidenced by the Paper read by the Bishop of Bath and Wells at the Church Congress held at Portsmouth in the autumn of last year. See *The Times*' report, October 7th, 1885. The Bishop's words were, "That task, let me repeat it, was to represent *in good English*, as exactly as we could, the meaning of Holy Scripture." * * * "Our responsibility was confined to expressing *in good English* the natural meaning of the Hebrew words."

Specimens of the Revisers' "*good English*," or what they considered to be such, will be found in the following pages.

# CHAPTER II.

CONTENTS.—The German revision of Luther's Bible. Orthographical errors; 'stories', for 'storeys'; 'builded', and 'built'; 'dwelled', and 'dwelt'; 'drave', and 'drove'; 'afore', and 'before'; 'astonied', and 'astonished'; 'aught', and 'ought'; 'naught', and 'nought'; 'strong hold', and 'stronghold'; 'a theist', and 'atheist'; compound words, 'firstripe', 'storehouse', 'brokenhearted', 'stargazers', 'cankerworm', 'pruninghooks', 'grapegatherers'; 'rams' skins', and 'sealskins'; 'deceased', for 'dead'; 'apparelled', for 'clothed'; 'augmenteth', for 'increaseth'; 'stablished', and 'established'; 'minished', and 'diminished'; 'prevent', and 'let', their double meanings; 'tell', to count; 'hardly', its two meanings; 'omer', and 'homer'; 'strewed', 'strawed', and 'strowed'; 'an hairy man', and 'a hairy man'; 'an hairy garment', and 'a hairy mantle'; 'chiefest', and 'higher than the highest'; 'stole', and 'stole away'; 'take'; 'gathered'; 'wax pale', and 'gather blackness'; the oneness of colour, Darwinism, the gender of earth and of sea, the myth of Hermaphroditos; 'handmaids'; 'annul', and 'disannul'; 'loose', and 'unloose'.

The Germans are now engaged in revising Luther's Bible, and have issued what they call a *Probe-bibel,* or a tentative revision of the Scriptures. They have adjourned for two years; at the end of which time they will meet again to rë-examine their work in the light of the abundant criticisms which they have invited from the press.

This is the course of action which eleven years ago (see *The Times* of May 22nd, 1875) I suggested to the English Revisers; but, for reasons best known to themselves, they ignored the suggestion. The public, however, will not accept as final any revision which leaves in the Bible such errors and inconsistencies as those which I shall expose.

Let us begin with orthography and etymology, and afterwards take up syntax.

We read, in Gen. vi. 16, of there having been "*stories*" in the ark; a spelling which might, to some minds, suggest the idea that Noah and his family had provided themselves with a little light literature for rainy days.

Modern usage discriminates between "*story*", a tale, and "*storey*", the flat of a building, by spelling the latter with an *e* before the *y*; and words so spelt make their plural by the addition of an *s* to the singular—*storey, storeys;* and not by changing the *ey* into *ies;* that form of the plural appertains to only those words which end in *y* immediately preceded by a consonant.

"*Story*", a tale, from the Gr. ἱστορία, a history, was formerly spelt "*storie*"; see '*Manipulus Vocabulorum*', by Peter Levins, 1570; and the plural of that spelling would be what the plural of *story* is, namely *stories*, which is the spelling adopted by the Revisers in speaking of the floors or stages in the ark. They should, of course, have written *storeys*.

I am aware that the word is written "*stories*" in the Authorised Version; but what was the object of the revision in regard to archaisms? Was it not to remove those which might lead to misunderstanding?

There are many inconsistencies in the Revisers' spelling. For instance, they say that Noah "*builded*" an altar, Gen. viii. 20; and that Abram "*built*" an altar, Gen. xiii. 18:

and that Solomon both "*builded*" and "*built*" the house of the Lord, 2 Chron. vi. 18 and 33.

This latter inconsistency is entirely the Revisers' own invention; it is not found in the corresponding passages in the Authorised Version.

Again, why do the Revisers say that Lot "*dwelled*" in the cities of the plain, Gen. xiii. 12, and say, that Abram "*dwelt*" by the oaks of Mamre, Gen. xiii. 18?

Why have we to read that the Israelites "*drave*" not out the Canaanites, Josh. xvi. 10; but "*drove*" out the Amorites, Num. xxi. 32; and "*drave*" out the three sons of Anak, Judges i. 20?

Why have we, "*afore*" in 2 Kings xx. 4; and "*before*", with the same signification, in the verse immediately preceding it, 2 Kings xx. 3?

Why have we, in the Revised Version, sometimes the word "*astonied*", and sometimes "*astonished*"? And, if it is a matter of indifference which we have, why did the Revisers alter "*astonished*" to "*astonied*" in Isa. lii. 14;

Jer. xiv. 9; and Ezk. iii. 15; and leave the word unaltered in a dozen other passages?

Reference to Dan. iv. 19, and viii. 27, will show that Daniel was both "*astonied*" and "*astonished*"; and so must those persons be who study the English of the Revisers.

Very properly, the Revisers have, in every instance, spelt the noun "*aught*" with an *a*; but, very improperly, they have spelt its negative, "*naught*", with an *o*; except in 2 Kings ii. 19 and Prov. xx. 14.

Why the Revisers made exceptions of those passages, and of those only, we have yet to learn.

"*Aught*" means "*anything*"; and its negative is "*naught*", "*nothing*".

"*Ought*" means "*owe*", of which it is the old preterite and past participle, and implies obligation; its negative would be "*nought*"; but we have no such word, though we have what looks like the adjective derived from it, "*naughty*", and if so, it should, in strictness, be spelt "*noughty*"; the meaning being "*not-ought-y*"; i.e., not in accordance with obligation or duty.

While speaking of the proper spelling of words, let me ask the Revisers why they have made two distinct words of the compound word " *stronghold* ", and said in Zech. ix. 3,

" Tyre did build herself a *strong hold*."

There is a right use of each form, which may be illustrated thus,

" He had a *stronghold* on the sea-coast; and his native land had a *strong hold* on his affections."

These forms are not interchangeable. Would the Revisers write " *a theist* " for " *atheist* " ?

If the Revisers did not act from caprice in repeatedly making two distinct words of the one word " *stronghold* ", why did they single out that word for division, and leave as compounds the words "*firstripe*", Micah vii. 1 ; "*storehouse*", Mal. iii. 10; "*brokenhearted*", Isa. lxi. 1; "*stargazers*", Isa. xlvii. 13 ; "*cankerworm*", Nah. iii. 15 ; "*pruninghooks*", Micah iv. 3 ; "*grapegatherers*", Jer. xlix. 9, &c. ? Why have they written " *rams' skins* " as two words;

and, in the very same verse, "*sealskins*" as one word? See Ex. xxxv. 23. It is not so in the Authorised Version.

The Revisers have, in general, wisely refrained from altering the character of the language of the Authorised Version; but here and there we find a few Latinisms introduced; fortunately they are but few, for they contrast very unfavourably with the simple Saxon words which they supplant.

For instance, in Psa. lxxxviii. 10, instead of

"Shall *the dead* arise and praise thee?"

we have now,

"Shall *they that are deceased* arise and praise thee?"

In Psa. xciii. 1, instead of

"The Lord reigneth; He is *clothed* with majesty",

we have now,

"The Lord reigneth; He is *apparelled* with majesty",

and yet, in Psa. civ. 1, we have,

"Thou art *clothed* with honour and majesty."

Surely, if the grander word "*apparelled*" is more needed in one passage than in the other, it is in the latter, where the Almighty is spoken of as being clothed "with honour" as well as with majesty.

Again, in Prov. xxviii. 8, instead of

"He that *increaseth* his substance",

we have now,

"He that *augmenteth* his substance";

both Latinisms, but the latter the more unusual, and therefore the less simple of the two. But why have the Revisers changed the word at all? Is not "*increase*" to augment? and is not "*augment*" to increase?

In Psa. xciii. 1, 2, in the Authorised Version, we read,

"The world also is *established*. . . . . thy throne is *established*";

but, in the Revised Version, the former of

these (and why the former, rather than the latter, or why either of them, it is impossible even to guess) is changed to "*stablished*"; so that now, in two consecutive verses, we read that the world is "*stablished*", and God's throne is "*established*".

What, I ask, is the supposed difference in the meaning of the two words, that the Revisers thought it needful to substitute one for the other in one instance? I know of none: "*stablished*" is from the L. "*stabilio*"; and "*established*" is from the same root through the old French "*establir*".

Another question which we may ask, but ask in vain, is, Why have the Revisers written, in verse 8 of Ex. v.,

"Ye shall not *diminish* aught";

and, in verse 19 of the same chapter,

"Ye shall not *minish* aught";

the reference in each passage being to the same transaction?

The meaning of words changes with the

lapse of time. The word "*prevent*" now means to obstruct; but, formerly, it had no such meaning. It is from the L. *prævenio*, to precede; and in that sense is used in the Church prayer,

"*Prevent* us, O Lord, in all our doings";

a rather strange prayer to be offered up to God by those persons who know only the modern signification of the word. The Revisers have altered it in Psa. lxxxviii. 13. In the Authorised Version it is,

"In the morning shall my prayer *prevent* thee."

In the Revised Version it is,

"In the morning shall my prayer *come before* thee."

But why do we read, in the Revised Version, Psa. cxix. 147,

"I *prevented* the dawning of the morning, and cried."?

"How is it possible to *prevent* the dawning

of the morning?" an uneducated man might ask. The Psalmist's meaning was, evidently, that his cry, or prayer, *preceded* the dawn. Why did not the Revisers make that meaning plain?

The Revisers speak of Jezebel's head being "*tired*", see 2 Kings ix. 30; they meant "*attired*", but the word which they have used sounds very like a joke, and reminds me of the reply which a coachman made to a passenger who had remarked to him that the horses seemed tired, " Yes, Sir ", said he, " they are tired, *and so are the wheels.*"

Another word which has now a meaning different from that which it had, is " *let* "; or rather, I should say, that of the two words " *let* ", which formerly were in use—the one from the Saxon " *lœtan* ", to loose, to let go, to allow; and the other from the Saxon " *lettan* ", to hinder,—only the former has continued to the present day. The other, though in common use in Shakspeare's time, would not be recognized in the English of the nineteenth century; and were we to read in any modern composition,

> "I'll make a ghost of him that *lets* me";
> *Hamlet*, Act 1, *Scene* iv.

we should naturally understand the writer to mean that the speaker would make a ghost of him that *allowed* him to do so; whereas Hamlet's words meant that he would make a ghost of him that *hindered* him. This is shown by the words immediately preceding;—

> "Unhand me, gentlemen!"

All this is perfectly familiar to the Revisers, yet they have left unaltered Isa. xliii. 13, where the word "*let*" means "*hinder*"; the passage reads as follows,

> "I am he; and there is none that can deliver out of my hand: I will work, and who shall *let* it?"

It should be,

> "I will work; and who shall *hinder* it?"

Another word which might with advantage have been changed, is the verb to "*tell*", in the sense of to "*count*". That meaning of the word is obsolete; yet it has been left, in Jer. xxxiii. 13, thus,

> "In the places about Jerusalem, and in the cities of Judah, shall the flocks again pass under the hands of him that *telleth* them."

The word has been left in Psa. lvi. 8, also,

> "Thou '*tellest*' my wanderings;"

and in Psa. cxlvii. 4,

> "He *telleth* the number of the stars;"

likewise in 1 Kings viii. 5,

> "Sheep and oxen, that could not be *told* nor numbered for multitude."

But in 2 Kings xii. 11, the Revisers have altered the word, and thereby have rendered the passage intelligible to all. In the Authorised Version it is,

> "And they gave the money, being *told*, into the hands of them that did the work."

In the Revised Version it is,

> "And they gave the money that was *weighed out* into the hands of them that did the work."

But why did the Revisers limit the alteration to this one solitary passage?

Great care is needed in using any word that has two meanings, lest it should be understood in a sense different from that which was intended.

The word "*hardly*" is such a one; and its two meanings are almost the opposites of each other. It means "*severely*", and it means also "*scarcely*".

In Job xix. 3, of the Revised Version, we read,

> "Ye are not ashamed that ye deal *hardly* with me."

Here, probably, the word means "*severely*"; but in the Authorised Version we read,

> "Ye are not ashamed that ye make yourselves strange to me";

in other words, "that ye *hardly* deal with me".

It is remarkable that these two renderings embody the two meanings of the word.—

> "Ye deal hardly [*severely*] with me."
> "Ye hardly [*scarcely*] deal with me."

Ought we to say "*an omer*", "*a homer*", or "*an homer*"? The Revisers give us the choice of all three. The first occurs in Ex. xvi. 16; the second in Isa. v. 10; and the third in Ezk. xlv. 11.

Should we say "*strewed*", "*strawed*", or "*strowed*"? The Authorised Version has "*strawed*" in Ex. xxxii, 20; this the Revisers have altered to "*strewed*"; yet in 2 Chron. xxxiv. 4, have written "*strowed*".

The anomalous character of the Revisers' work is its most striking feature, and will constitute the chief subject of remark in these criticisms. There appears to have been no comprehensive supervision of the Revisers' labours, having for its object the consistency and homogeneousness of the whole. Not infrequently the teaching of a judicious alteration correcting an error in one place is rendered nugatory by an alteration in exactly the opposite direction elsewhere; so that a student cannot possibly determine, from the work before him, which is right, and which is wrong.

Should we speak of "*an* hairy man", or "*a* hairy man"? The former expression is found in 2 Kings i. 8; the latter in Gen. xxvii. 11; and if we should say "*a* hairy man", why "*an* hairy garment", Gen. xxv. 25? and if "*an* hairy garment", why "*a* hairy mantle", Zech. xiii. 4?

If the trumpet give an uncertain sound, who shall prepare himself for the battle? 1 Cor. xiv. 8., and if the Revisers show that they did not know their own minds, who can have confidence in their judgment?

There are many minor errors which I gladly pass over; but I must speak of the Revisers' persistent use of the word "*chiefest*": see 1 Sam. ii. 29; ix. 22; xxi. 7; and Cant. v. 10; a fourfold repetition of a word that conveys an untruth! It affirms that the chief is not chief; in fact, that there is a "higher than the highest"; and yet—will it be believed?—the Revisers, with their usual inconsistency, have corrected that very error in Eccl. v. 8.

It is not in good taste, to say the least of it,

to insert in the Bible such plays upon words as the following appear to be.

> "Rachel *stole* the teraphim that were her father's. And Jacob *stole away*." Gen. xxxi. 19, 20.
>
> "*Take*, I pray thee, my gift, . . . and he *took* it. And he said, Let us *take* our journey." Gen. xxxiii. 11, 12.
>
> "He *gathered* up his feet into the bed, and yielded up the ghost, and was *gathered* unto his people." Gen. xlix. 33.
>
> "I was not rebellious, neither turned away *backward*. I gave my *back* to the smiters." Isa. l. 5, 6.

Neither is it in good taste to speak of faces "*waxing*" pale, seeing that the word "*wax*" has two meanings.

By-the-bye, that reminds me of two of the strangest alterations to be found in the Revised Version of the Old Testament. See Joel ii. 6; and Nahum ii. 10. In the Authorised Version we read,

> "All faces shall *gather blackness*."

In the Revised Version it is

"All faces are *waxed pale*."

Is black, then, really white? and is it true that colour has no existence? I am aware that this has long been the theory of physicists; and now it seems to have the sanction of the most eminent divines; but I must say that their way of recording their sanction is rather droll. However, the fact that they do hold the belief of the oneness of all colour receives confirmation from their rendering of Ex. xxxv. 23, where they say,

"And every man, with whom *was* found blue, and purple, and scarlet, and fine linen, and goats' hair, and rams' skins dyed red, and sealskins, brought them."

But surely this theory of "*oneness*", based on the fact that the verb is in the singular, proves too much; and yet/I do not know that it does; for it may be that the Revisers intended to indicate their approval of the Darwinian doctrine of the original oneness of all animals also; for here we have goats, rams, and seals;

and the verb referring to them, as well as to the colours, is in the singular.

The investigation of the Revisers' language is certainly fraught with much interest; and the careful student of it will meet with many surprises; as, for instance, when he reads, in Gen. iv. 12, that the earth is both neuter and feminine. But the most astounding surprise will be that which he will experience when he regards collectively Ezk. xxxi. 4, Hab. iii. 10, and Rev. xx. 13.

Talk of the Greek myth of Hermaphroditos! That is far surpassed by the Revisers' account of the mighty deep, which, they tell us, is at once feminine, masculine, and neuter.

Moreover, here is a mysterious affair/ Bilhah and Zilpah still were maids though they had each borne Jacob two sons; at least, so the learned Revisers say. See Gen. xxxii. 22, where the expression "women-servants" has deliberately been altered to "handmaids".

Why do the Revisers use the word "*dis-annul*"? The preferable word is "*annul*", which means to reduce to nothing, to make void or of no effect. "*Disannul*" appears to mean its very opposite, and therefore is misleading, when the Revisers use it in the sense of "*annul*". See Job xl. 8;

> "Wilt thou even *dis*annul my judgment?"

In Isa. also, xiv. 27, we read,

> "The Lord of hosts hath purposed, and who shall *dis*annul it?"

Again, in Isa. xxviii. 18, we read,

> "Your covenant with death shall be *dis*annulled, and your agreement with hell shall not stand."

A similar incongruity in our language exists with regard to the word "*unloose*". If to "*loose*" means to liberate, does to "*un*loose" mean to make fast? The word is not in the Bible, neither should "*dis*annul" be found there.

## CHAPTER III.

CONTENTS.—Verbs, violation of the rules governing them; knowledge and wisdom, their difference; 'people', singular and plural; 'multitude', singular and plural; 'persons'; 'peoples'; 'kings', singular, and 'gods', plural; 'flesh and heart', singular, and 'heart and flesh', plural; sequence of events governs the order of their relation; 'lightning and thunder', not 'thunder and lightning'; angels 'descending and ascending', not 'ascending and descending'.

Having briefly glanced at the Revisers' errors in orthography and etymology, let us now look at their syntax; and knowing that in every sentence the verb is, as its name implies, *the word, par excellence,* we will begin with that.

The first rule respecting it, is that it shall agree with its nominative. The Revisers, however, treat with lofty disdain all rules of grammar; and yet, occasionally, they seem to have had a twinge of conscience concerning their violations of some of them, and a consciousness of the offence likely to be given by such a course; for here and there we see evidence of their having "trimmed their way to seek love", by altering a passage to make it in accordance with what, I suppose, they call popular prejudice.

Some years ago I read, before the Royal Society of Literature, a Paper entitled "*Common Errors in Speaking and Writing*"; and in it I called attention to certain violations of grammar occurring in the Authorised Version of the Scriptures. A copy of the Paper was sent to the Revisers; and they have corrected some of the errors which I pointed out. For instance, in Ex. ix. 31, the Authorised Version reads,

"The flax and the barley *was* smitten."

I stated that this is equivalent to saying "*they was*". The Revisers, very properly, have altered it to,

"The flax and the barley *were* smitten."

Again, in Lam. iii. 47, in the Authorised Version, we read,

> "Fear and a snare *is* come upon us".

This the Revisers have altered to,

> "Fear and the pit *are* come upon us".

Though what they mean by "*the pit*" coming upon us, I cannot imagine.

See also Prov. i. 27. The Authorised Version has,

> "When distress and anguish *cometh* upon you."

In the Revised Version it has been corrected thus,

> "When distress and anguish *come* upon you."

Why, then, after altering the verb to agree with its nominative in the foregoing passages, have the Revisers left uncorrected such errors as the following?

> "Wisdom and knowledge *is* granted unto thee." 2 Chron. i. 12.

> "Thy wisdom and thy knowledge, *it hath* perverted thee." Isa. xlvii. 10.

Do the Revisers hold that wisdom and knowledge are one? Let the poet Cowper explain to them the difference:—

> "Knowledge and wisdom, far from being one,
> Have ofttimes no connection; knowledge dwells
> In heads replete with thoughts of other men,
> Wisdom, in minds attentive to their own."

Perhaps the Revisers consider wisdom as nothing, and therefore have taken no account of it; for I see that elsewhere when mention is made of it in conjunction with a noun other than knowledge, they still put the verb in the singular; e.g.,

> "Thy wisdom and prosperity exceed*eth* the fame which I heard." 1 Kings x. 7.

See likewise Dan. v. 11,

> "Understanding and wisdom *was* found in him."

and Dan. v. 14,

> "Understanding and excellent wisdom *is* found in thee."

The same singularity occurs in Job. xii. 13,

" With him *is* wisdom and might."

This apparent ignoring of the existence of wisdom is much to be regretted. The Revisers would have found a little more of it very useful to them.

Sometimes the Revisers, in their uncertainty as to which is right, give both singular and plural verbs to the same nominative in the same verse. This plan has at least one advantage—it ensures that the Revisers shall for once be right, though with the disadvantage that they shall also once be wrong.

In Gen. xli. 48, we are told that,

> "Joseph gathered up all *the food* of the seven years *which were* in the land of Egypt, and laid up the food in the cities: *the food* of the field, *which was* round about every city, laid he up in the same."

Perhaps the Revisers meant

> "the food (of *the field which was* round about every city) laid he up in the same";

but the passage really means,

> "*the food of the field* (which was round about every city) laid he up in the same."

The Revisers' error is in the earlier part of the verse. They ought not to have said,

> "*the food* . . . which *were* in Egypt."

See also Isa. viii. 6,

> "Forasmuch as this people *hath* refused the waters of Shiloah that go softly, and *rejoice* in Rezin and Remaliah's son."

Is "*people*" singular, or plural, in this verse? If singular, "*rejoice*" is wrong; if plural, "*hath*" is wrong.

The same confusion of singular and plural with regard to "*people*" occurs in Jer. iv. 22; v. 23; vii. 16; viii. 5; xiv. 11; xviii. 15; l. 6; and elsewhere.

In Judges ix. 33, we read of

> "The people that *is*";

and, in the very next verse, this singular people is made plural, and we read of

> "The people that *were*".—Judges ix. 34.

The word "*people*" seems to have sorely troubled the Revisers; evidently they did not know what to do with it. In Num. xiii. 18, we read,

> "See the land, what it is; and the people that *dwelleth* therein, whether *they* be strong or weak."

But, in verse 28 of the same chapter, it is no longer,

> "the people that *dwelleth*";

but,

> "the people that *dwell*".

Yet, in each instance, the word "*people*" refers to the same inhabitants, the possessors of the land of Canaan.

See likewise Isa. ix. 13,

> "The people *hath* not turned unto him that smote *them*, neither *have they* sought the Lord of hosts."

I cannot but express my surprise at the Revisers' persistent inconsistency. They carefully altered, twice over, the phrase

> "all the people that *was*",

(see Ex. xix. 16; and 2 Sam. xv. 30;) to

"all the people that *were*";

and yet in 2 Chron. xxxii. 7, they leave the phrase

"all the multitude that *is*".

The Revisers cannot plead that they were bound by the Hebrew verb; for the verb is not expressed in the Hebrew. In Lev. viii. 4, we have

"The congregation *was* assembled".

But in Num. xvi. 3, "congregation" is plural,

"All the congregation *are* holy."

By way of contrast to 2 Chron. xxxii. 7, the Revisers give us, in Isa. v. 13,

"their multitude *are*".

In Job xxxvi. 20, the Revisers have altered "*people*" to "*peoples*"; but I think that there, "*persons*" would have been a better rendering. In ordinary parlance, the word "*people*" is often misused for "*persons*"; e.g., we hear it said,

> "There were three *people* present."

The error here will be apparent if you ask yourself what the result would be if two of those "*people*" were to leave. Would there be *one people* present? The passage in Job is as follows:

> "Desire not the night,
> When peoples [*persons*] are cut off in their place."

The Revisers' alteration of "*people*" to "*peoples*" is in most instances judicious; and I think it would have been as well to make that alteration in 1 Kings x. 15 also. The passage there is,

> "All the kings of the mingled *people*".

Surely, as there were "*kings*", it should have been "*peoples*".

I have said that in the Hebrew of 2 Chron. xxxii. 7, the verb is not expressed; nor is it in any of the following score of passages. Therefore the blame of putting the verb in the singular while the nominative to it is in the plural, in these several passages, rests entirely on the Revisers.

> "Thy going out and thy coming in with me in the host *is* good." 1 Sam. xxix. 6.
>
> "Thy silver and thy gold *is* mine; thy wives also and thy children, . . . *are* mine." 1 Kings xx. 3.
>
> "With them *was* Jozabad the son of Jeshua, and Noadiah the son of Binnui." Ezra viii. 33.
>
> "His power and his wrath *is* against all them that forsake him." Ezra viii. 22.
>
> "My petition and my request *is*". Esther v. 7.
>
> "With him *is* strength and effectual working; The deceived and the deceiver *are* his." Job xii. 16.
>
> "With God *is* my salvation and my glory." Psa. lxii. 7.
>
> "The inward thought of every one, and the heart, *is* deep." Psa. lxiv. 6.
>
> "There *is* no breaking in, and no going forth." Psa. cxliv. 14.

> "There *is* precious treasure and oil." Prov. xxi. 20.
>
> "Before me continually *is* sickness and wounds." Jer. vi. 7.
>
> "Where *is* corn and wine?" Lam. ii. 12.
>
> "There *was* written therein lamentations, and mourning, and woe." Ezk. ii. 10.
>
> "The meal offering and the drink offering *is* withholden." Joel i. 13.
>
> "Unto the Lord thy God *belongeth* the heaven, and the heaven of heavens, the earth, with all that therein is." Deut. x. 14.
>
> "Thine, O Lord, *is* the greatness, and the power, and the glory, and the victory, and the majesty." 1 Chron. xxix. 11.

In the following passage we have "*is*" for "*are*", and "*are*" for "*is*";

> "Where *is* thy zeal and thy mighty acts? *the yearning* of thy bowels and thy compassions *are* restrained toward me." Isa. lxiii. 15.
>
> "Where *is* the king of Hamath, and the king of Arpad, and the king of the city of Sepharvaim, of Hena, and Ivvah?" 2 Kings xix. 13.

Read 2 Kings xviii. 34; and Isa. xxxvi. 19; there we have,

> "Where *are* the gods of Hamath, and of Arpad? Where *are* the gods of Sepharvaim, of Hena, and Ivvah?"

Why are "*kings*" singular, and "*gods*" plural?

> "There *is* tidings in his mouth." 2 Sam. xviii. 25.

Compare this with Ex. xxxiii. 4; there the word "*tidings*" is plural;

> "*These* evil tidings."

Again,
> "Out of his mouth *cometh* knowledge and understanding." Prov. ii. 6.

In the previous chapter, Prov. i. 27, we have,
> "When distress and anguish *come* upon you";

but, in the Authorised Version, it is "*cometh*". Why did the Revisers correct the latter, and leave the former uncorrected?

> "My flesh and my heart *faileth*." Psa. lxxiii. 26.

Why did the Revisers leave this error, yet correct a parallel one in Psa. lxxxiv. 2 ? There, in the Authorised Version, it is

"My heart and my flesh *crieth* out for the living God";

but, in the Revised Version, it has been corrected to,

"My heart and my flesh *cry* out".

In Prov. v. 11, also, we have,

"Thy flesh and thy body *are* consumed";

therefore, their leaving uncorrected the passage in Psa. lxxiii. 26, is the more inexcusable.

There are, in the Revised Version, many other passages where the verb does not agree with its nominative. I will give a few of them.

"There *was* hail, and fire mingled with the hail." Ex. ix, 24.

"Thy silver and thy gold *is* multiplied." Deut. viii. 13.

"Ahaz took the silver and gold that *was* found." 2 Kings xvi. 8.

"On the fourth day *was* the silver and the gold and the vessels weighed." Ezra viii. 33.

"Even as the gazelle and the hart *is* eaten." Deut. xii. 22.

"Only in the Lord, shall one say unto me, *is* righteousness and strength." Isa. xlv. 24.

"This one and that one *was* born in her." Psa. lxxxvii. 5.

"Violence and spoil *is* heard in her." Jer. vi. 7.

"His right hand, and his holy arm, *hath* wrought salvation." Psa. xcviii. 1.

"My graven image, and my molten image, *hath* commanded them." Isa. xlviii. 5.

"The vine, and the fig tree, and the pomegranate, and the olive tree *hath* not brought forth." Hag. ii. 19.

"There *was* given him dominion, and glory, and a kingdom," Dan. vii. 14.

"Gladness and joy *is* taken away."—Jer. xlviii. 33.

Why are "*gladness and joy*" singular, and "*anguish and sorrows*" plural, as they are in the following chapter, Jer. xlix. 24? Will the

Revisers say that the verb is governed by the noun nearest to it, and that "*joy*" is singular, and "*sorrows*" plural, and therefore the verbs are respectively singular and plural? That is plausible, but not logical. The nominative to the singular verb is not "*joy*", but "*gladness and joy*"; therefore the verb should be plural, to agree with its nominative.

Besides, if the verb is governed by the noun immediately preceding it, why did the Revisers write, in Job xv. 21,

"A sound of *terrors is* in his ears"?

They knew very well that the nominative to the verb is "*sound*", and not "*terrors*"; and that therefore the verb had to be in the singular. See, likewise, Job xxi. 21,

"The number of his *months is* cut off."

Here the nominative to the verb is "*number*", and not "*months*"; and therefore here also the verb had to be in the singular. Again,

"The rain *cometh* down and the snow from heaven, and return*eth* not thither, but water*eth* the earth, and mak*eth* it bring forth and bud, and giv*eth* seed to the sower." Isa. lv. 10.

It would be grammatically correct to write thus of either the rain *or* the snow; but it is not allowable to write thus of the rain *and* the snow.

"The remnant of Jacob shall be in the midst of many peoples as dew from the Lord, as showers upon the grass; that tarri*eth* not for man, nor wait*eth* for the sons of men." Micah v. 7.

Here "tarri*eth*", being singular, seems to refer to "*grass*", and therefore is misleading, because it really refers to "*showers*"; and that being plural, the verbs "*tarrieth*" and "*waiteth*" also ought to have been plural, to agree with it.

"Mine anger and my fury *hath* been poured forth." Jer. xlii. 18.

"My fury and mine anger *was* poured forth, and *was* kindled." Jer. xliv. 6.

Not only is the verb wrong here, but the sequence of events is wrong: the kindling must have preceded the pouring forth, and therefore should have been mentioned first. Events should be recorded in the order of their occurrence.

For this reason we ought not to speak of "*thunder and lightning*", but of "*lightning and thunder*"—the cause first, the effect afterwards. The Revisers have erred in this matter also, see Ex. xx. 18,

> "And all the people saw the thunderings, and the lightnings, and the voice of the trumpet."

How they "*saw*" the "*thunderings*" and the "*voice*", I cannot conceive; there is evidently some mistranslation here.

I suppose that the reason why the thunder is generally spoken of before the lightning, is that it is the more impressive of the two. Indeed, by ignorant persons, it is often thought to be the cause of the damage that is really done by the lightning. I remember once, when on a walking tour in Normandy, speaking to a poor old man respecting a tree that had been struck by the lightning. But the old man could not agree with me that it was the lightning which had caused the destruction: "*Mais non, Monsieur; c'etait le tonnerre,*" were his words.

Another instance of the Revisers' non-observance of the order of sequence is found in Gen. xxviii. 12, where we read,

> "And he dreamed, and behold a ladder set up on the earth, and the top of it reached to heaven: and behold the angels of God *ascending* and *descending* on it."

As the angels' abode is in heaven (Matt. xviii. 10) they must have *descended*, before they could *ascend*. However, it was a dream; and events are often strangely transposed in dreams.

Let us return to the consideration of the Revisers' errors with respect to verbs. The Revisers may say that, in some of the passages which I have quoted, the verb has been put in the singular because, although there are in the nominative two nouns joined by the conjunction "*and*", the two really are one; e.g., "*fury*" and "*anger*"; "*rain*" and "*snow*", which is rain in another form. But will the Revisers call "*evil*" and "*good*" one? Surely not; yet, in Lam. iii. 38, we read,

> " Out of the mouth of the Most High com*eth* there not evil and good ?"

Again, in Jer. vi. 20, we read,

> "To what purpose com*eth* there to me frankincense from Sheba, and the sweet cane from a far country ?"

Compare this with Prov. xxvii. 9; there we read,

> " Ointment and perfume *rejoice* the heart."

How is it that the Revisers consider "*ointment and perfume*" plural, and "*frankincense and sweet cane*" singular ?

In 2 Kings xxv. 5, we are told that

> "The army of the Chaldeans pursued after the king, and overtook him in the plains of Jericho; and all his army *was* scattered from him";

but in verse 10 of the same chapter we are told that

> "All the army of the Chaldeans, that *were*

with the captain of the guard, brake down the walls of Jerusalem ".—2 Kings xxv. 10.

Now, in the name of common sense, I ask why the Revisers have made "*all the army*" of the Jews singular; and, in the same chapter, "*all the army*" of the Chaldeans plural?

This inconsistency does not exist in the Authorised Version; there both verbs are plural. Why did the Revisers create this anomaly?

I am afraid that I ask in vain: their inconsistency baffles all conjecture as to its cause, and its object.

# CHAPTER IV.

CONTENTS.—Perspicuity; 'harlots unto the king'; men 'oppressed with their own flesh'; order of words in a sentence; errors of omission, virtually errors of commission; 'in her tongue' (i.e. 'in her speech'), erroneously altered to 'on her tongue.'

By way of varying our study of the English of the Revisers, let us for a while turn from their errors in grammar, and look at their arrangement of the sequence of their words; a matter which we slightly glanced at in the previous chapter.

Perspicuity, which is of primary importance in literary composition, depends very greatly on this. Indeed the collocation of the words may be said to govern the meaning.

In 1 Kings iii. 16, we read,

"Then came there two women, that were harlots, unto the king, and stood before him."

Do the Revisers mean that in Solomon's days there were women who held the appointment of "*harlots, unto the king*"? It cannot be! Why, then, did not the Revisers, by arranging the sequence of their words as follows, guard against the suggesting of such a thought?

> "Then came there, unto the king, two women that were harlots."

In 2 Chron. xxviii. 6, we read,

> "Pekah the son of Remaliah slew in Judah an hundred and twenty thousand in one day, all of them valiant men; because they had forsaken the Lord, the God of their fathers."

Here, again, the sequence of the words is bad; for it might lead to the inference that the hundred and twenty thousand were " all valiant men because they had forsaken the Lord, the God of their fathers."

A very slight transposition and change of the words was needed, to avoid this error. The Revisers should have said,

> "Pekah the son of Remaliah slew in Judah in one day, a hundred and twenty thousand valiant men, because they had forsaken the Lord, the God of their fathers."

In Isa. xlix. 26, we read,

> "I will feed them that oppress thee with their own flesh."

What does this mean? Does it refer to such persons as Eglon, the King of Moab, who was a very fat man? Judges iii. 17. Their flesh may certainly be said to oppress others besides oppressing themselves. But probably the Revisers meant nothing of the sort, but meant,

> "I will *feed with their own flesh* them that oppress thee; and they shall be drunken with their own blood."

Then why did not the Revisers say so? It was easy enough. In Dan. ix. 17, we read,

> "Hearken unto the prayer of thy servant, and to his supplications, and cause thy face to shine upon thy sanctuary that is desolate, for the Lord's sake."

Was the sanctuary "*desolate, for the Lord's sake*"? Certainly not; therefore the Revisers should have said

> "And, for the Lord's sake, cause thy face to shine upon thy sanctuary that is desolate."

Besides, by this arrangement, not only is the meaning made clear, but the most emphatic word in the sentence comes last, where it will be the most impressive:—

> "Thy sanctuary that is *desolate*"!

Of course I am speaking as if the words had been addressed to man, and not to God. But in our addresses to Heaven, we should "set our words in order", Job xxxiii. 5, and not be rash with our mouth nor let our hearts be hasty "to utter anything before God." Eccl. v. 2.

Again, in Gen. xxxix. 5, 6, we read,

> "The Lord blessed the Egyptian's house . . . . and he left all that he had in Joseph's hand."

The Revisers do not mean what the words

affirm, viz., that the Egyptian left "all that he had in Joseph's hand"; but that

> "He left in Joseph's hand all that he had."

In Jer. xxx. 2, we read,

> "Write thee all the words that I have spoken unto thee in a book."

The words were not spoken unto him in a book. The Revisers should have said,

> "Write thou in a book all the words that I have spoken unto thee."

In Gen. vi. 17, we read,

> "Behold, I do bring the flood of waters upon the earth, to destroy all flesh, wherein is the breath of life, from under heaven."

This is a very badly arranged sentence. It would read better thus,

> "Behold I bring upon the earth the flood of waters to destroy from under heaven all flesh wherein is the breath of life."

In Ex. xxvi. 14, we read,

> "And thou shalt make a covering for the tent of rams' skins dyed red."

The Revisers did not mean to speak of a "*tent of rams' skins dyed red*", for which some kind of a covering was ordered to be made; therefore they should have said,

> "And thou shalt make for the tent a covering of rams' skins dyed red."

The error is repeated in Ex. xxxvi. 19.
In Ex. xxv. 22, we read,

> "There I will meet with thee, and I will commune with thee from above the mercy-seat, from between the two cherubim which are upon the ark of the testimony, of all things which I will give thee in commandment unto the children of Israel."

This should have been,

> "There I will meet with thee, and from above the mercy seat, from between the two cherubim which are upon the ark of the testimony, I will commune with thee of all things which I will give thee in commandment unto the children of Israel."

The Revisers' sentence is faulty because two

parts of it, which are most intimately connected in sense, are separated by eighteen intervening words; with the result that, instead of our reading,

"I will commune with thee of all things",

we read of,

"The ark of the testimony, of all things".

Once more; in Isa. lix. 21, we read,

"This is my covenant with them, saith the Lord: my spirit that is upon thee, and my words which I have put in thy mouth, shall not depart out of thy mouth, nor out of the mouth of thy seed, nor out of the mouth of thy seed's seed, saith the Lord, from henceforth and for ever."

Here, in the latter part of the sentence, the words "*saith the Lord*" are redundant, as they occur in the former part of it; but, if, for emphaticness, it was thought necessary to repeat them, they should have followed the words "*from henceforth and for ever*", seeing that those words refer, not to the expression "*saith the Lord*", but to the eternity of God's covenant with his people. The passage, then, should have been written thus,

> "This is my covenant with them, saith the Lord: my spirit that is upon thee, and my words which I have put into [not "*in*"] thy mouth, shall not depart out of thy mouth, nor out of the mouth of thy seed, nor out of the mouth of thy seed's seed, from henceforth and for ever, saith the Lord."

Frequently the Revisers' errors are those of omission; but as the duty which the Revisers undertook was that of thorough revision of the Scriptures, the errors of omission become errors of commission; for by perpetuating those of the former translators (or what by changes in our language have virtually become errors) the Revisers have made them their own, and are equally responsible for them and for those which they themselves have introduced.

The following, however, is not an error of omission, but of commission; the error consisting in not leaving the passage as it stood in the Authorised Version, Psa. xvii. 7.

| Authorised Version. | Revised Version. |
|---|---|
| "Shew thy marvellous loving-kindness, O thou that savest by thy right hand them which put their trust in thee from those that rise up against them." | "Shew thy marvellous lovingkindness, O thou that savest them which put their trust in thee. From those that rise up against them, by thy right hand." |

The Revisers' version of the passage makes God's right hand the means by which the wicked rise against the righteous. But the Bible distinctly says that God will not help evil-doers, or, as the margin reads,

"Will not take the ungodly by the hand." Job. viii. 20.

There is, in the Authorised Version of the Book of Proverbs (xxxi. 26), a beautiful description of the language of a virtuous woman; and one of the charms of the passage is the delicate balancing of its different parts. Compare the two versions, the Authorised and the

Revised, and you will see how the harmony of the whole has been destroyed by the Revisers' alteration of it.

| *Authorised Version.* | *Revised Version.* |
|---|---|
| "She openeth her mouth with wisdom; and in her tongue is the law of kindness." | "She openeth her mouth with wisdom; And the law of kindness is on her tongue." |

The Revisers have altered "*in* her tongue" to "*on* her tongue"; but here likewise, they are wrong; for, "*tongue*" in this passage does not mean the organ of taste; it means that which is spoken by the "*tongue*", L. *lingua*, the tongue, whence our word "*language*". Therefore the Authorised Version is correct in saying,

"And *in* her tongue [i.e., *in* her language, not *on* it] is the law of kindness."

This is a very absurd error. Besides, if it should be "*on* her tongue" here, why should it be "*in* my tongue" in Psa. cxxxix. 4?

Moreover, in the Authorised Version, each clause of the passage is divided into two parts, beautifully balanced in expression and meaning:

"She openeth her mouth—with wisdom ;
And in her tongue is—the law of kindness."

In the Revised Version, the transposing of the last clause destroys the balance of the parts, mars the melody of the whole, and removes from the place of emphasis the word "*kindness*", which should have been left at the end of the sentence, that it might linger in the ear, and dwell undisturbed in the memory.

# CHAPTER V.

CONTENTS.—The letter H, 'hairy and 'airy'; 'a' and 'an'; 'a eunuch'; 'an hiatus'; 'such a one,' and 'such an one'; 'no end' and 'none end'; 'my' and 'mine'; 'thy' and 'thine'; 'thy honour.'

What were the Revisers' opinions of the use of the letter "H"? In the Authorised Version, we read, in Num. xxx. 6, of "*an* husband"; this, in the Revised Version, has been altered to "*a* husband". So also, in Ex. xxviii. 32, "*an* hole" has been altered to "*a* hole"; and, in Lev. xxiii. 12, "*an* he-lamb" has been altered to "*a* he-lamb". But, as if to neutralize this teaching, "*a* harlot" has been altered to "*an* harlot", in Joel iii. 3.

Again, in Neh. vii. 5, "*mine* heart" has been altered to "*my* heart"; and, in 1 Chron. xvii. 16, "*mine* house" has been altered to "*my* house". Did the Revisers make this latter alteration because they knew that the "*h*" being asperated in "*house*", the pronoun should be "*my*" and not "*mine*"? or was it because they thought it probable that "*mine* house" might be so pronounced as to be mistaken for "my νους", and each Reviser's modesty forbade his even seeming to speak of *that*?

In Dan. iv. 10, "*mine* head" has been altered to "*my* head"; and, in 2 Sam. i. 25, "*thine* high places" has been altered to "*thy* high places"; while in Ex. xviii. 4, "*mine* help" has been altered to "*my* help". But, as if to neutralize this correction also, "*my* helper" has been altered to "*mine* helper" in Psa. liv. 4.

In 2 Chron. xxv. 19, "*thine* hurt" has been altered to "*thy* hurt"; but, as if this also had to be neutralized, and, for some mysterious purpose, students of English had to be bewildered, the Revisers have altered "*my* hurt" to "*mine* hurt", in Psa. xxxv. 26.

However, I will do my best to neutralize the Revisers' teaching, by showing that, in the matter of English scholarship, they are but blind leaders of the blind. Let none follow them.

With regard to the letter "*H*", why have certain of the foregoing errors been corrected, and a hundred others similar been left? What excuse have the Revisers for giving us the following archaisms, some of which are not found in the corresponding passages in the Authorised Version?

"*An* help". Gen. ii. 18, 20.
"*An* hundred". Gen. viii. 3.
"*An* husbandman". Gen. ix. 20.
"*An* heifer". Gen. xv. 9.
"*An* handmaid". Gen. xvi. 1.
"*An* heap". Gen. xxxi. 46.
"*An* house". Gen. xxxiii. 17.
"*An* harlot". Gen. xxxiv. 31.
"*An* haven". Gen. xlix. 13.
"*An* hoof". Ex. x. 26.
"*An* hired servant". Ex. xii. 45.
"*An* high hand". Ex. xiv. 8.
"*An* holy nation". Ex. xix. 6.
"*An* handbreadth". Ex. xxv. 25.

## ECCLESIASTICAL ENGLISH.

"*An* heave offering". Ex. xxix. 28.
"*An* hin of wine". Ex. xxix. 40.
"*An* handful". Num. v. 26.
"*An* heart". Deut. v. 29.
"*An* hammer". Judges iv. 21.
"*An* hair-breadth". Judges xx. 16.
"*An* helmet". 1 Sam. xvii. 5, 38.
"*An* half". 1 Kings vii. 31.
"*An* horse". 1 Kings xx. 20.
"*An* host". 2 Kings vi. 15.
"*An* hissing". 2 Chron. xxix. 8.
"*An* hedge". Job i. 10.
"*An* hidden birth". Job iii. 16.
"*An* heinous crime". Job xxxi. 11.
"*An* heavy burden". Psa. xxxviii. 4.
"*An* haughty spirit". Prov. xvi. 18.
"*An* honeycomb". Prov. xvi. 24.
"*An* healer". Isa. iii. 7.
"*An* harp". Isa. xvi. 11.
"*An* habitation". Isa. xxii. 16.
"*An* hungry man". Isa. xxix. 8.
"*An* hill". Isa. xxx. 17.
"*An* hiding place". Isa. xxxii. 2.
"*An* hart". Isa. xxxv. 6.
"*An* horrible thing". Jer. xxiii. 14.
"*An* hard language". Ezk. iii. 5, 6.

"*An* horn". Ezk. xxix. 21.
"*An* harvest". Hosea vi. 11.
"*An* herdman". Amos vii. 14.
"*An* howling". Zeph. i. 10.

That the practice of the Revisers is, in this matter, as in many others, inconsistent, will be seen from the following quotations :—

"*An* hundred". Num. ii. 24.
"*A* hundred". 1 Chron. xxix. 7.
"*An* holy one". Dan. iv. 23.
"*A* holy one". Dan. viii. 13.
"*An* he-goat". Dan. viii. 5.
"*A* he-lamb". Lev. xxiii. 12.
"*An* hammer". Judges iv. 21.
"*A* hammer". Jer. xxiii. 29.
"*An* homer". Ezk. xlv. 11.
"*A* homer". Lev. xxvii. 16.
"*An* husband". Deut. xxii. 22.
"*A* husband". Num. xxx. 6.
"*An* harp". Isa. xxiii. 16.
"*A* harp". 1 Sam. x. 5.
"*An* high wall". Prov. xviii. 11.
"*A* high wall". Isa. xxx. 13.

"*An* hard language". Ezk. iii. 5, 6.
"*A* hard thing". 2 Kings ii. 10.
"*An* hairy garment". Gen. xxv. 25.
"*A* hairy mantle". Zech. xiii. 4.
"*An* hairy man". 2 Kings i. 8.
"*A* hairy man". Gen. xxvii. 11.

Can any one tell me why the Revisers have described Esau as "*a* hairy man", and Elijah as "*an* hairy man"? Was it because it was considered that, in Elijah's case, the "*h*" should be dropped, "'airy" being a more appropriate description of him who "went up by a whirlwind into heaven"? 2 Kings ii. 11. For my own part, I consider such jokes as quite out of place in the Bible. Let us, then, leave this specimen of lack-wisdom clerical *levity* (no pun intended), and resume our criticisms.

Another matter, intimately connected with the use of "*a*" and of "*an*" before "*h*", is the proper use of "*an*" before words beginning with a vowel.

It is apparent that the Old Testament Revisers believed it to be correct to put "*an*" before all words beginning with a vowel, and that the New Testament Revisers held a contrary opinion; for, in the Revised Version of Jer. xxxviii. 7, we read of "*an* eunuch"; but in Acts viii. 27, the expression "*an* eunuch" has been altered to "*a* eunuch", in the Revised Version. Here the Old Testament Revisers are wrong, and the New are right, because the rule is, not that "*a*" becomes "*an*" before a vowel, as erroneously taught by Lindley Murray, but that "*a*" becomes "*an*" before a vowel sound in order to avoid an hiatus; the change being purely for the sake of euphony.

The phrase which I have just now employed, "*an hiatus*", is a good example of this; for, the emphasis being on the second syllable, the aspiration of the "*h*" is suppressed, and the result is the production of a vowel sound, at the beginning of the word, necessitating the employment of "*an*", instead of "*a*", which latter would have been needed had the "*h*" been fully aspirated.

Now, in the word "*eunuch*", the "*e*" has the

sound of "*y*", and that being a consonant, when used at the beginning of a word, should be preceded by "*a*", and not by "*an*"; we should say "*a* eunuch", not "*an* eunuch".

For the same reason we ought not to say, as the Revisers have said,

> "Such *an* one". Job xiv. 3; Psa. l. 21; and lxviii. 21;

but "such *a* one", as they, with their usual inconsistency, have said in Ruth iv. 1.

It is as incorrect to say "such *an* one", as it would be to say, "such *an* wonder".

In Ezk. xvi. 5, we read,

> "*None eye* pitied thee";

but in Job x. 18; and xxiv. 15, it is

> "*No eye*".

Why this difference?

In Nahum ii. 9, and iii. 3, we read,

> "There is *none end*";

but in Isa. ix. 7; Psa. cii. 27; Eccl. iv. 8, 16; and xii. 12, it is "*no end*".

Why this difference?

In Zeph. ii. 5, we read,

> "*No* inhabitant";

but in the very next chapter, Zeph. iii. 6, it is,

> "*None* inhabitant".

Why this difference?

"*None*" is an abbreviation of "*no one*", and occurs in both forms in Isa. xxxiv. 16:—

> "Seek ye out the book of the Lord, and read : *no one* of these shall be missing, *none* shall want *her* mate."

It is singular, and is so used a hundred times in the Bible. What reason, then, had the Revisers for using it as a plural in 1 Kings x. 21, saying,

> "All the vessels were of pure gold: *none were* of silver";

and, in 2 Chron. ix. 11, also,

> "There *were none* such seen before"?

In Jer. xxxiv. 9, 10, the Revisers make it both singular and plural,

"*None* should serve *himself*", and "*None* should serve *themselves.*"

Certainly the Revisers' consistency is worthy of honourable mention.

Let us continue our criticisms, and we shall see additional reasons for this.

"*Thine* hand". Deut. ii. 24 } same chapter.
"*Thy* hand". Deut. ii. 7

"*Thine* head". Gen. xl. 13 } same chapter.
"*Thy* head". Gen. xl. 19

"*Thine* handmaid". 2 Sam. xiv. 7, 17 } same chapter.
"*Thy* handmaid". 2 Sam. xiv. 6, 15

"*Thine* house". Ruth iv. 11; 2 Sam. xi. 10.
"*Thy* house". Ruth iv. 12; 2 Sam. xi. 8.
                same chapters.

"*Thine* heart". 2 Kings x. 15; 1 Sam. xiv. 7.
"*Thy* heart". 2 Kings x. 15; 1 Sam. xiv. 7.
                same verses.

"*Thine* heart". Lam. ii. 19 } same verse.
"*Thy* hands". Lam. ii. 19

"*Thine* husband". Num. v. 20 } same verse.
"*Thy* husband". Num. v. 20

"*Thine* horn". Micah iv. 13 } same verse.
"*Thy* hoofs". Micah iv. 13

"*Thine* estimation". Lev. xxvii. 27 } same verse.
"*Thy* estimation". Lev. xxvii. 27

"*Thine* enemies". Deut. xxxiii. 29 } same verse.
"*Thy* excellency". Deut. xxxiii. 29

"*Thine* exactors". Isa. lx. 17 } same verse.
"*Thy* officers". Isa. lx. 17

"*Thine* ox". Ex. xxiii. 12 } next verse.
"*Thy* oliveyard". Ex. xxiii. 11

"*Mine* holy things". Ezk. xliv. 8 } same chapter.
"*My* holy things". Ezk. xliv. 13

"*Mine* heart". Psa. cxix. 112 } same psalm.
"*My* heart". Psa. cxix. 161

"*Mine* affliction". Psa. cxix. 92 } same psalm.
"*My* affliction". Psa. cxix. 50

"*Mine* house". Isa. lvi. 7 } same verse.
"*My* house". Isa. lvi. 7

"*Mine* hand". 1 Sam. xxiv. 11 } same verse.
"*My* hand". 1 Sam. xxiv. 11

"*Mine* head". Psa. xl. 12 } same verse.
"*My* heart". Psa. xl. 12

"*Mine* hand". Isa. xlix. 22 } same verse.
"*My* ensign". Isa. xlix. 22

"*Mine* husband is dead". 2 Sam. xiv. 5.
"*My* husband is dead". 2 Kings iv. 1.

In Prov. xx. 3, the Revisers say "*an* honour"; but in Psa. lxxi. 8, they say "*thy* honour"! But let me "render honour to whom honour is due", Rom. xiii. 7; and candidly express my opinion that, notwithstanding these vagaries, it is evident that the Revisers had some sense of propriety in dealing with the personal pronouns; for, in an address to an *ass*, (Num. xxii. 29) we find the asinine expression "*mine* hand"; but, in the previous chapter, in an address to the *Deity*, the expression is "*my* hand". (Num. xxi. 2).

Doubtless the Revisers had equally good reasons for all their varieties of expression; and some day they will, for the enlightenment of mankind, publish those reasons; but, in the mean time, the Revisers' light being, as it were, hid under a measure, is in a measure hid.

# CHAPTER VI.

CONTENTS. — Redundancy, 'vomit them up again'; 'doubled twice'; 'budded buds and bloomed blossoms'; 'plaister it with plaister'; 'pitch it with pitch'; 'praying a prayer'; 'kneeling on his knees'; 'stood on his feet'; 'heard with our ears'; 'see it with thine eyes'; 'devised devices'; 'assembled together'; 'a widow woman whose husband is dead'; 'stone him with stones'; 'rise up'; 'vanish away'; 'depart away'; 'no doubt but'; 'all of them'; 'each of them'; 'both of them'; 'both of those, both of four, both of five, both of eight, and of things innumerable; 'else'; 'it".

One of the commonest faults in the language of young writers and inexperienced public speakers is redundancy. Having no confidence in the power of simple expressions, they trust to iteration and reïteration, rather than to one incisive utterance that would instantly pierce the understanding. Their speech is more like the repeated dull blows of a hammer on the head of a blunt nail, than the lightning flash of intellect which cleaves the surrounding darkness;' and, by its dazzling brilliancy, at once and for ever photographs itself upon the mind.

And, as with youthful writers, so it is with languages which, in the world's history, may be said to be youthful. This is true of the Hebrew language especially; it is extremely elliptical; but, at the same time, it abounds with tautologies and other redundancies; and this fact, having unfortunately been allowed by the Revisers to have undue weight in their choice of words, has given rise to some of the following redundant expressions.

> "*Of* the tree of the knowledge of good and evil, thou shalt not eat *of it*". Gen. ii. 17.
>
> "Is there room *in* thy father's house for us to lodge *in?*" Gen. xxiv. 23.
>
> "He *restored* the chief butler unto his butlership *again*." Gen. xl. 21.

As the butler had not previously been restored, he could not be said to have been restored *again*. Why, then, did the Revisers leave in this passage the word "*again*", seeing that they struck it out of Lev. xxiv. 20, where, in the Authorised Version, a similar redundancy occurs.

See also 1 Kings xiii. 6,

> "And the man of God intreated the Lord, and the king's hand was restored him *again*."

Had the king's hand been restored previously? If not, how could it be said to have been restored *again*?

In Ex. xiv. 26, we read,

> "Stretch out thine hand over the sea, that the waters may come *again upon the Egyptians*".

A comma after the word "*again*" might improve this sentence, but it would be still more improved by the omission of that word. As the sentence stands now, one is tempted to ask, "Had the sea on some former occasion overwhelmed the Egyptians?"

In Gen. xli. 32, we read,

> "The dream was doubled unto Pharaoh twice."

A perusal of the chapter will show that the dream of Pharaoh was *doubled*, but not doubled *twice;* he did not dream the same circumstances four times.

I have said that "*some*" of the redundancies are found in the Hebrew. They are not all there; e.g., the redundancy of the word "*again*", in Num. xii. 14 and 15, has no equivalent in the Hebrew.

In Job xx. 15, we read,

> "He hath swallowed down riches, and he shall vomit them up *again*".

This is a very unpleasant metaphor; for, before anything can be vomited *again*—I will say no more; only that the original does not mean what the Revisers' language implies.

In Ex. xiv. 13, we read,

> "The Egyptians whom ye have seen to-day, ye shall see *them* again no more *for ever*."

Omit the words in Italics: "*them*" is redundant, "*Egyptian*" being the accusative to the verb; and the phrase "*for ever*" is worse than redundant, for it implies that the Israelites had previously seen the Egyptians "*for ever*"! but should do so "*again* no more".

In Ex. iii. 5, and Josh. v. 15, we read,

> "Put *off* thy shoes from *off* thy feet".
> "The rod of Aaron was *budded*, and put forth *buds*, and *bloomed blossoms*". Num. xvii. 8.
> "Whosoever toucheth the *dead body* of any man that is *dead*". Num. xix. 13.
> "Thou shalt set thee up great stones, and *plaister* them with *plaister*." Deut. xxvii. 2, 4.
> "Rooms shalt thou make in the ark, and shalt *pitch* it within and without with *pitch*." Gen. vi. 14.
> "*Then Solomon assembled* the elders of Israel . . . . . *unto king Solomon*". 1 Kings viii. 1.
> "When Solomon had made an end of *praying* all this *prayer*, he arose from *kneeling* on his *knees*." 1 Kings viii. 54. See also, Dan. vi. 10.
> "Then David the king stood up *upon his feet*. 1 Chron. xxviii. 2.

Did the Revisers imagine that we should think he stood upon his head?

In Job xxviii. 22, we read,

> "We have heard a rumour thereof *with our ears*."
>
> "Behold, thou shalt see it *with thine eyes*". 2 Kings vii. 2; Deut. xxxiv. 4.
>
> "Hear, O Lord, when I cry *with my voice*". Psa. xxvii. 7.
>
> "I knew not that they had *devised devices* against me". Jer. xi. 19; See also, xviii. 18; Dan. xi. 25.

In the Authorised Version of this last passage, it is "they shall *forecast devices*", but the Revisers preferred to be literally tautological, and therefore altered the passage.

In Dan. vi. 11, we read,

> "Then these men *assembled together*, and found Daniel making petition."

How could they assemble otherwise than "*together*"? But, evidently the Revisers imagined it possible, or they would not have inserted the word "*together*"; they would have given us the passage as it stands in the Authorised Version, viz.,

> "Then these men assembled, and found Daniel praying".

The error is repeated in verse 15.

Here is a fine specimen of tautology:

> "Of a truth I am a widow *woman, and* mine husband is dead." 2 Sam. xiv. 5.

Why do the Revisers speak of a "widow *woman*"? Do they think it likely that any one would imagine that the "*widow*" was a man? And then, as if they had not been sufficiently explicit in telling us that the widow was a woman, they must needs add "*and* my husband is dead". Surely, the death of the husband is implied in the word "*widow*". But, if they wished to be emphatic, they might with propriety have said,

> "Of a truth I am a widow,—my husband is dead!"

The error occurs also in 1 Kings xi. 26, and xvii. 9.

In Ex. xii. 33, we read,

> "The Egyptians were urgent upon the people, to send them out of the land in haste; for they said, We be all dead *men*."

The equivalent to the word "*men*" is not in the original; why, then, have the Revisers inserted it in the English of the passage? There can be no question that the Egyptians' remark referred, not to the "*men*" only, but to the whole nation. It was called forth by the death of "all the firstborn in the land of Egypt", and therefore certainly had reference to children as well as to men.

In Lev. xx. 2, we read,

> "The people of the land shall *stone* him with *stones*."

Why this tautology? Could he be *stoned* with any thing else? In verse 16, of chapter xxiv., it says simply,

> "All the congregation shall certainly stone him."

So also, in 1 Sam. xxx. 6, the expression is simply,

> "The people spake of stoning him."

.

But in the following passages it is "*stoning with stones*": Lev. xxiv. 23; Num. xiv. 10; xv. 35, 36; Deut. xiii. 10; xxi. 21; xxii. 21, 24; Josh. vii. 25; 1 Kings xii. 18; xxi. 13; 2 Chron. x. 18; xxiv. 21; and Ezk. xvi. 40.

In Deut. xix. 2, we read,

> "Thou shalt separate three cities for thee in the midst of thy land, *which* the Lord thy God giveth thee to possess *it*."

If the Revisers thought the word "*it*" to be necessary in the foregoing passage, why did they omit it in the following verse, Deut. xix. 3? There we read,

> "Thou shalt prepare thee the way, and divide the borders of thy land, *which* the Lord thy God causeth thee to inherit."

Why not "inherit *it*"? There is just as much, or as little, need of the word "*it*" in the one case as in the other. The same error occurs in Deut. xxi. 1 and Josh. i. 11.

In 1 Sam. i. 13, we read,

> "Now Hannah, *she* spake in her heart; only

her lips moved, *but* her voice was not heard".

Here the word "*she*" is redundant, as "*Hannah*" is the nominative to the verb "*spake*". The word "*but*" likewise is redundant; the word "*only*" rendering it needless. The passage should have been,

" Now Hannah spake in her heart; only her lips moved, her voice was not heard."

In Psa. xliv. 26, we have,

" Rise *up* for our help".

Why "rise *up*"; is it possible to rise *down?* In the Authorised Version it is,

"*Arise* for our help."

This is called "*revising*"!

In Isa li. 6, we read,

"The heavens shall vanish *away* like smoke".

See also Job vii. 9,

"As the cloud is consumed and vanisheth *away*".

And Zech. x. 11, we read,

> "The sceptre of Egypt shall depart *away*."

Again, 2 Kings ii. 11, we read,

> "There appeared a chariot of fire, and horses of fire, which parted them *both* asunder".

How much more forcible these passages would be if the redundant words which I have italicized, were omitted.

In Job xii. 1, 2, we read,

> "Then Job answered and said,
> No doubt *but* ye are the people".

The insertion of the redundant word "*but*" in this sentence, really makes Job say exactly the reverse of what it is evident that he intended; namely,

> "There is no doubt *that* ye are the people".

The Revisers' words mean that there is no doubt *except* that they are the people; there *is* doubt about that.

"*But*" is from the Saxon "*be-utan*"; originally the imperative of "*beon-utan*," to be out.

It is literally "*be out*", and means "*exclude*" or "*except*".

The same error occurs in Gen. xxiii. 6, where we read,

> "None of us shall withhold from thee his sepulchre, *but* that thou mayest bury thy dead."

Substitute "*except*" for "*but*", and you will at once see that its presence in the passage reverses the meaning of the speaker.

> "None of us shall withhold from thee his sepulchre, *except* that thou mayest bury thy dead."

i.e., we will withhold it for that; but the speaker's intention was, we will give it for that.

The word "*but*" should be omitted; the meaning then will be obvious,

> "None of us shall withhold from thee his sepulchre, that thou mayest bury thy dead."

In Deut. xxix. 10, we read,

"Ye stand this day *all of you* before the Lord your God".

In Lev. x. 1, we read,

"Nadab and Abihu, the sons of Aaron, took *each of them* his censer".

In Jer. xlvi. 12, we read,

"They are fallen *both of them* together."

And in Prov. xvii. 15, we read,

"*Both of them* alike are an abomination to the Lord."

Why have the Revisers inserted the words "*of them*" in each of the last two passages? In the Authorised Version of the passages the words are not found, nor are they needed. These are additional instances in which the Revisers have made faulty that which was correct.

"*Both*" is *all* of two; but "*of them*" is partitive, and therefore implies that something is left. Hence the incongruity; for, when all is gone, how can anything be left?

The expression "*both of them*" occurs in

Gen. xxii. 6, 8; Ex. xxxvi. 29; Lev. xx. 11, 12, 13, 18; 1 Sam. ii. 34; Prov. xx. 10, 12; and twelve times in the seventh chapter of Numbers; but it is as incorrect as is "*all of them*", and that for the same reason. Yet the Revisers have used that expression in Deut. xxxiii. 17; 1 Chron. vii. 3; 2 Chron. v. 12; Ezra viii. 20; Isa. vii. 19; Ezk. vii. 16; xx. 40; and Amos ix. 1.

In speaking of *all*, the words "*of them*", "*of these*", "*of you*", "*of us*", are worse than redundant. It is sufficient to say "*all*", "*both*", or "*each*". The more sententious we make our language, the more forcible will it be.

In Deut. xxiii. 18, the Revisers use the correct form, and say, not "both *of* these", but,

"*Both these* are an abomination unto the Lord thy God."

"*Both*" means "*the two*"; yet the Revisers have used it in reference to *three*, in Judges xx. 48,

"And smote them with the edge of the

sword, *both* the entire city, and the cattle, and all that they found".

•In the Authorised Version it is,

"And smote them with the edge of the sword, *as well* the men of every city, as the beast, and all that came to hand".

Therefore this error, in using "*both*" in reference to *three*, rests solely with the Revisers.

In Gen. vi. 7, the Revisers have used the word "*both*" in reference to *four;* so have they in Num. xxxi. 28, where we read,

"Levy a tribute unto the Lord [,] of the men of war that went out to battle: one soul of five hundred, *both* of the persons, and of the beeves, and of the asses, and of the flocks".

In the Hebrew of this passage, there is no equivalent to the word "*both*". Why, then, have the Revisers inserted it? and if they deemed it to be needful in this verse, why was it not needful in the verse next but one also, Num. xxxi. 30, where it is not found, though the expressions are almost identical? It reads thus,

>"Take one drawn out of every fifty, of the persons, of the beeves, of the asses, and of the flocks".

In Joshua vi. 21, and Neh. xii. 27, the Revisers use the word "*both*" when speaking of *five* things. And in 1 Sam. xv. 3 they use the word when speaking of *eight* things!

>"Slay both man and woman, infant and suckling, ox and sheep, camel and ass."

I suppose the Revisers mean, "*both* man and woman, *both* infant and suckling, *both* ox and sheep, *both* camel and ass." But why use the word "*both*"? It adds nothing to the meaning, and is therefore redundant.

I have shown that the Revisers use the word "*both*" when speaking of *three*, of *four*, of *five*, and of *eight* different things. Now turn to Gen. vii. 21, and you will see that the Revisers there use it in reference to things *innumerable*.

>"All flesh died that moved upon the earth, *both* fowl, and cattle, and beast, and *every*

creeping thing that creepeth upon the earth, and every man ".

And yet in Ex. xxxv. 25, and xxxvii. 26 they have corrected the error! Truly they are persistently consistently inconsistent.

In Neh. ii. 2, we read,

> "Why is thy countenance sad, seeing thou art not sick? this is nothing *else* but sorrow of heart".

"*Else*" is equivalent to the Latin "*alius*", and means "*other*"; therefore, in such sentences as that which I have quoted, it should be followed by "*than*", not by "*but*". The Revisers should have said,

> "This is nothing *else than* sorrow of heart";

or they might have omitted the word (and there is nothing in the Hebrew justifying its presence in the sentence) and have said,

> "This is nothing *but* sorrow of heart".

A similar error occurs in Judges vii. 14,

> "This is nothing *else save* the sword of Gideon."

In Prov. xxvi. 4, we read,

> "Answer not a fool according to his folly,
> Lest thou *also* be like unto him".

If this sentence had had reference to other persons who had answered a fool according to his folly and had become like him; and the person addressed were cautioned against doing as they had done, then the word "*also*" would have been permissible. But there is no evidence in the context that any such reference was intended; therefore the "*also*" is redundant, and the passage should have read thus,

> "Answer not a fool according to his folly,
> Lest thou become like him."

In Isa. xxxiv. 16, we read,

> "Seek ye out the book of the Lord, and read: no one of these shall be missing, none shall want her mate: for my mouth *it* hath commanded, and his spirit *it* hath gathered them."

Compare this with the following passage, from Isa. xlviii. 5, and conceive, if you can, why the Revisers have sanctioned the pronominal tautology in the former, and have avoided it in the latter:

> "Mine idol hath done them, and my graven image, and my molten image, hath [have] commanded them."

If the former passage is correct, the latter should have been,

> "Mine idol *it* hath done them, and my graven image and my molten image *they* have commanded them."

This might have been in accordance with Hebrew idiom; but it would certainly not have been good English.

The same error occurs in Prov. x. 22,

> "The blessing of the Lord, *it* maketh rich";

and in Prov. x. 24,

> "The fear of the wicked, *it* shall come upon him."

But I need not multiply instances of this kind of error; numerous examples of it can be found by any superficial reader of the Revised Version; and even to those who have become accustomed to this construction, a moment's reflection will show it to be a fault.

In one instance the Revisers have struck out the word "*it*" from a verse of this description in the Authorised Version; I refer to Prov. xix. 2,

> "That the soul be without knowledge, *it* is not good."

Their selection of this verse, as the one to be altered, was not judicious; almost any other would have done better; for the presence of the word "*it*" might by some persons be justified on the ground that, if the last clause of the sentence be transposed and put first, the word "*it*" must be retained, thus:

> "*It* is not good that the soul be without knowledge".

therefore,

> "That the soul be without knowledge, *it* is not good."

I should not write it so; but the reasoning is plausible.

Why do the Revisers speak of a woman's "*latter end*"? e.g.:

> "Her filthiness was in her skirts; she remembered not her *latter end*". Lam. i. 9.
> "Oh that they would consider their *latter end!*". Deut. xxxii. 29.
> "Thy *latter end* should greatly increase." Job. viii. 7.
> "The Lord blessed the *latter end* of Job". Job xlii. 12.
> "He shall not see our *latter end.*" Jer. xii. 4.
> "Let my *last end* be like his." Num. xxiii. 10.

The Revisers' language implies that the end to a man's existence may be elsewhere than at the close; otherwise, why speak of the "*latter end*" and "*last end*"?

## CHAPTER VII.

CONTENTS.—The articles, 'a', 'an', and 'the'; 'another'; 'the other'; 'the son of man', or 'a son of man'; the verb 'to be'; the subjunctive mood.

The Revisers' errors are not such as are occasionally found in the writings of advanced students of the language—errors in the structure of complex sentences—there we might reasonably expect the Revisers to fail; for, very few Englishmen write their own language with accuracy. The marvel is, that the Revisers, besides failing in other things, fail in the simple A B C of the grammar, the proper use of "*a*", "*an*", and "*the*"!

I have, on pages 63-70, given some examples of this; here are some more.

Every one knows that "*an*" is indefinite, and refers indiscriminately to one of several; and that "*the*" is definite, and refers specially to one by itself, which may be a single unit, or which may be an aggregate of units; yet the Revisers say, in Dan. v. 6,

> "Then the king's countenance was changed in him, and his thoughts troubled him: and the joints of his loins were loosed, and his knees smote one against *an*other."

This statement might be correct if Belshazzar had three or more knees, and it was uncertain which of the knees "smote one against another." But as history does not say that he had more than two legs (though his father did eat grass like an ox) the Revisers are not justified in writing as if he had more than two knees; and therefore ought to say that

> "his knees smote one against *the* other."

The difference between "*an*" and "*the*" cannot have a better illustration than the one found in Ezk. vii. 2,

> "*An* end, *the* end is come."

That the Revisers were aware of the propriety of employing the definite article "*the*", when speaking of only two things, is evident from their having altered "*an*other", as it is in the Authorised Version, to "*the* other", in the Revised Version. See Gen. xv. 10,

> "He took all these, and divided them in the midst, and laid each half over against *the* other."

Why, then, after thus acknowledging the necessity for the alteration, have the Revisers left the error in Gen. xxxi. 49, and elsewhere?

> "The Lord watch between me and thee, when we are absent one from *an*other."

It should be,

> "When we are absent, one from *the* other."

In Ex. xxv. 18, 20; and xxxvii. 9, we read,

> "And thou shalt make two cherubim of gold; .... And the cherubim shall spread out their wings on high, covering the mercy-seat with their wings, with their faces one to *an*other."

In 1 Kings vi. 23, 27, we read,

> "In the oracle he made two cherubim of olive wood, .... and their wings touched one *an*other." See also Ezk. i. 11.

In Ezk. xxxvii. 16, 17, we read,

> "Take thee [thou] one stick, and write upon it, For Judah, . . . . then take another stick, and write upon it, For Joseph, . . . and join them for thee one to *an*other".

In Ex. xxvi. 17, we read,

> "Two tenons shall there be in each board, joined one to *an*other." See also Ex. xxxvi. 22.

In Ezk. iv. 4-8, we read,

> "Thy left side . . . . thy right side . . . . Thou shalt not turn thee from one side to *an*other".

In each of the foregoing passages, the Revisers should have said, not "*an*other", but "*the* other". And in the following passages, they should have said, "*each* other", instead of "one *an*other".

> "Then Amaziah sent messengers to Jehoash . . . . saying, Come, let us look one *an*other in the face". 2 Kings xiv. 8, 11, and 2 Chron. xxv. 17, 21.

In the Authorised Version there occurs the following reading:—

"Thy righteousness may profit *the* son of man".
Job. xxxv. 8.

This the Revisers have with great prudence altered to,

"Thy righteousness may profit *a* son of man".

The expression "*son of man*" occurs nearly a hundred times in Ezekiel; but "*the*" Son of Man is one of the titles of Christ (see Psa. lxxx. 17; Matt. xvi. 13, &c.), and therefore it was that the Revisers recognized the necessity for making the above correction.

But, recognizing this necessity, why did they leave unaltered the same expression in Job xxv. 6, where we read that "the son of man" is a worm? and still more, why did they leave unaltered Psa. cxlvi. 3? There it says,

"Put not your trust in princes,
Nor in *the* son of man, in whom there is no help."

The Revisers should have said,

"Nor in *any* son of man".

The same error occurs in Num. xxiii. 19; Psa. viii. 4; cxliv. 3; Isa. li. 12; and lvi. 2.

The following passages are correct, Job xxxv. 8; Jer. xlix. 18, 33; l. 40; and li. 43.

In Lev. xvii. 3, we read of

"an ox, or lamb, or goat".

But in a sentence like this, where one of the nouns begins with a vowel, and each of the others begins with a consonant, it is especially necessary that the appropriate article precede each. The Revisers should have said,

"*an* ox, or *a* lamb, or *a* goat".

The sentence, as it stands in the Revised Version, means

"*an* ox, or [*an*] lamb, or [*an*] goat".

The Revisers have recognized this in Psa. lxix. 31. There, in the Authorised Version, we read,

"This also shall please the Lord better than an ox or bullock".

which is equivalent to saying

"*an* ox or [*an*] bullock".

In the Revised Version it is,

"*an* ox, or *a* bullock",

which is correct.

But how is it that we so frequently find that an error corrected in one part of the Revisers' work, is left uncorrected in another? There must have been something extremely faulty in their mode of revision.

I believe the explanation to be, that the Revisers were not all equally good masters of English; and as they were not always all present, and as everything was carried by votes of the majority, the less-informed were frequently the more numerous and therefore, of course, outvoted those who knew better.

In any further revision, this evil must be guarded against. The marvel is, that *any* educated men could have sanctioned the errors which I have exposed; or, at least, that they have considered them so unimportant that it was not deemed necessary to record a protest against them. Therefore even the best of the Revisers must be held to have been "partakers of other men's sins".

Even the simple verb "*to be*" meets with strange treatment at the hands of the Revisers. It cannot be that its various forms were not understood; and yet they seem to have puzzled the Revisers almost as much as they puzzled the Oriental lecturer, who ridiculing our English language, and especially the changeable verb "*to be*", said, "In my country, if *I am, I am* always". "Oh, well", said a reviewer, "if you *am* always in your own country, how *am* it that you *am* here? And if a man always *am*, what *am* he when he *am* not? And how *am* he to simplify or unify, as it *am*, our verb '*to am*', so that we shall always *am* here, as they *am* in Burmah? Somehow we *am* at a loss to see how this verb '*am*' *am*, with any success, to be reformed on a Burmese basis. How *am* this? Any way, 'to *am*, or not to *am*, that *am* the question'".

Let us look at the Revisers' treatment of the verb "*to be*". Their examples of its uses are certainly strange. Here are some of them,

> "There *be* three things which *are* too wonderful for me". Prov. xxx. 18. See also verses 24 and 29.
>
> "There *be* six things which the Lord hateth; Yea, seven which *are* an abomination unto him." Prov. vi. 16.

Could anything be more capricious?—"There *be* six, and there *are* seven". What has number to do with it? The inconsistency is not found in the corresponding passage in the Authorised Version. There we read,

> "These six things doth the Lord hate: yea, seven are an abomination unto him".

In Amos vi. 2 of the Revised Version we read,

> "*Be* they better than these kingdoms? or *is* their border greater than your border?"

Neither is this inconsistency found in the Authorised Version.

In Psa. xxxiv. 18, and cxxv. 4, we read,

"The Lord is nigh unto *them that are* of a broken heart,
And saveth *such as be* of a contrite spirit."
"Do good, O Lord, unto *those that be* good,
And to *them that are* upright in their hearts."

In these two verses we have the expressions "*them that are*"; but in Ezk. xxxi. 17, 18, the expression is "*them that be*"; and in the next chapter we have both forms,

"Them that *be* slain". v. 25.
"Them that *are* slain". v. 30.

Nor is this inconsistency found in the corresponding verses in the Authorised Version; (though it does exist elsewhere in that Version) neither is there in the Hebrew, in either verse, any equivalent to the expression "*them that be*" or "*them that are*". Why, then, have the Revisers altered the translation of the latter verse and not that of the former?

The same inconsistency exists in the following passages. See Ezk. xlii. 13,

> "The north chambers and the south chambers, *which are* before the separate place, *they be* the holy chambers".

Likewise, Ezk. xliii. 19,

> "Thou shalt give to the priests the Levites *that be* of the seed of Zadok, *which are* near unto me".

Also Zech. iv. 4, 5,

> "What *are* these my Lord? .... Knowest thou not what these *be?*"

See also Zech. i. 19,

> "What *be* these? And he answered me, These *are* the horns".

And Zech. iv. 11, 12,

> "What *are* these two olive trees? .... What *be* these two olive branches?"

And so on, *usque ad nauseam.* See Gen. xxxiv. 15 (compare with verse 22); xxxvi. 43 (compare with verse 15); xxix. 4; Num. xiii. 31; Deut. i. 1 (compare with Num. xxx. 16); x. 5; Judges viii. 5; 2 Sam. i. 5 (compare with verse iv.); xxiii. 1; Job iii. 17 (compare with verse 18); v. 11; &c.

For some reason the Revisers have corrected the following passages, Gen. xlvi. 15; Ex. vi. 14; Lev. x. 14; xi. 31; Num. iv. 45; xiii. 28; Deut. xxvii. 4; Judges xi. 26; 2 Sam. vii. 28; &c.

The Revisers' alteration of some passages, and of some only, shows the incompleteness of their work.

In '*The Revisers' English*' I discussed so fully the commission of errors in connection with verbs in the subjunctive mood, that it is not necessary to say much more than that the Revisers of the Old Testament are as faulty in that respect, as were those of the New. True, here and there the former seem to be groping after the correct form of expression; and occasionally they are right; but more frequently they are wrong. In Prov. xxix. 12, they say,

"If a ruler hearken*eth* to falsehood,
All his servants *are* wicked."

As the circumstance here spoken of relates to the present time, the Revisers very properly have taken the verb from the subjunctive, in which it stands in the Authorised Version, and have put it into the indicative.

But so likewise does 1 Kings ii. 23 refer to the present time; why, then, have the Revisers not put that also into the indicative? The verse reads thus,

> "God do so to me, and more also, if Adonijah *have* not spoken this word against his own life."

It should be,

> "if Adonijah *has* not spoken".

With a perverseness, at which one cannot but smile, the Revisers have, in the last quotation, put the verb into the subjunctive when it ought to be in the indicative, and in 1 Kings xvii. 14, have put the verb into the indicative when it ought to be in the subjunctive, the time being future. The words are,

> "The barrel of meal shall not waste, neither

shall the cruse of oil fail, until the day that the Lord send*eth* rain upon the earth."

It should be,

"until the day that the Lord *send* rain",

i.e., "until the day when the Lord [*shall*] send rain".

The general rule governing this form of speech is very simple; it is this:—"Where there is in the circumstance a combination of contingency and futurity, the verb must be in the subjunctive mood; but where there is either contingency without futurity, or futurity without contingency, the verb must be in the indicative mood."

In the following passages the time spoken of is certainly present, and therefore the verb should be in the indicative; yet the Revisers have put it into the subjunctive,

"If it *be* not so *now*". Job xxiv. 25.

This should be,

"If it *is* not so *now*".

Again, in Judges vii. 10, we read,

> "Arise, get thee down into the camp . . . But if thou *fear* to go down".

It should be,

> "But if thou fear*est* to go down".

Another example of this error will be found in Ex. xl. 37,

> "If the cloud *were* not taken up, then they journeyed not."

Here there is contingency, but not futurity; it is the relation of a past event, and therefore the Revisers should have said,

> "If the cloud *was* not taken up, then they journeyed not."

For other examples of the error, see Judges vi. 13, 31; 1 Kings xviii. 21; Neh. ii. 5; Esther vi. 13; viii. 5; Prov. xxiv. 10.

An example of the correct use of the indicative in a contingent sentence is found in Esther iv. 14,

> "If thou altogether hold*est* thy peace";

and an example of the correct use of the subjunctive in a contingent sentence is found in Num. xxx. 14,

"If her husband altogether *hold* his peace".

The former quotation relates to the present; the latter relates to the future; hence the necessity for the change of mood in the verb.

So simple; yet, apparently, so little understood!

# CHAPTER VIII.

CONTENTS.— Consistently inconsistent; adjectives and adverbs; 'speak plain', or 'speak plainly'; 'look sad', or 'look sadly'; 'wonderful great', and 'exceeding magnifical'; 'for to'; 'in', and 'into', 'on', and 'onto', 'on', and 'in'; prepositious; 'of', for 'by'; 'of', for 'on'; 'despite'.

I have spoken of the Revisers' inconsistency; but I wish to be strictly accurate, and therefore bear testimony to their consistency in one matter which I must admit never varies, and that is the maintenance of their *in*consistency.

Having disburdened my mind by the rendering of this act of justice to the Revisers, I proceed to show that their claims to this concession on my part are very great.

Compare the following passages with each other.

"Write upon the stones all the words of this law very plain*ly*." Deut. xxvii. 8:

"The tongue of the stammerers shall be ready to speak plain*ly*." Isa. xxxii. 4.

"His tongue was loosed, and he spake *plain*". Mark vii. 35.

"Say now Shibboleth; and he said Sibboleth; for he could not frame to pronounce it *right*." Judges xii. 6.

Surely the rule respecting the right use of adjectives and adverbs must have been forgotten by the Revisers; and if so, I do not wonder at their being puzzled which to employ; but then why did they not ask, rather than blunder, and bring disgrace on the language of Scripture?

The rule is, that if the verb is intended to denote the manner of doing a thing, an adverb should be used; but if the verb is intended to denote the nature or the quality of a thing, then an adjective should be used. Further, the appropriateness of using an adjective may be tested by our being able to substitute for the adjective so used, some part of the verb "*to be*"; for, the verb "*to be*" in all its moods and tenses, generally requires the word immediately connected with it, to be an adjective, not an adverb; consequently, when this verb can be substituted for any other without varying the sense or the construction, that other verb also must be connected with an adjective. Of course there are exceptions to this rule, but we should not reject a useful general rule because it is attended with exceptions.

In Gen. xl. 7, the Revisers make Joseph say to Pharaoh's officers,

"Wherefore look ye so sad*ly* to day?"

As Joseph's enquiry did not refer to the *manner* in which they looked, but to the *nature* of their looks, the verb should have been followed by an adjective, not by an adverb. The inquiry should have been,

"Wherefore look ye so *sad* to day?"

Test the correctness of this expression by substituting, for the verb "*look*", part of the verb "*to be*", and you will find the value of the rule.

"Wherefore *are* ye so *sad* to day?"

In Num. xxxvi. 5, we have,

"The tribe of the sons of Joseph speaketh *right*."

This is correct; because what was intended was not that they spoke in a proper *manner*, but that the *nature* of their request was *right*." Test the correctness of this sentence also by the substitution of part of the verb "*to be*" for the verb "*speaketh*".

"The tribe of the sons of Joseph *is* right.

The adjective "*exceeding*" is erroneously employed for the adverb "*exceedingly*" in numerous passages in the Revised Old Testament; e.g.,

"Exceeding great". Gen. xv. 1.
"Exceeding fruitful". Gen. xvii. 6.
"Exceeding mighty". Ex. i. 7.
"Exceeding strong". Ex. x. 19.
"Exceeding loud". Ex. xix. 16.
"Exceeding good". Num. xiv. 7.

"Exceeding many". 2 Sam. xii. 2.
"Exceeding much". 2 Sam. xii. 30.
"Exceeding guilty". Ezra. ix. 7.
"Exceeding broad". Psa. cxix. 96.
"Exceeding crooked". Prov. xxi. 8.
"Exceeding wise". Prov. xxx. 24.
"Exceeding deep". Eccl. vii. 24.
"Exceeding beautiful". Ezk. xvi. 13.
"Exceeding hot". Dan. iii. 22.
"Exceeding glad". Dan. vi. 23.
"Exceeding terrible". Dan. vii. 19.
"Exceeding magnifical". 1 Chron. xxii. 5.
"Wonderful great". 2 Chron. ii. 9.

Contrast the foregoing with the following,

"Then were the men exceeding*ly* afraid." Jonah i. 10.

"The queen was exceeding*ly* grieved." Esther iv. 4.

In this matter the Revisers are ten times as often wrong as they are right. May we not, in their own words, describe their errors as "*wonderful great*", and their language as "*exceeding magnifical*"?

The American company of Revisers suggested many very judicious emendations which unfortunately were not duly appreciated by the English Revisers. A list of those emendations is printed at the end of each division of the Scriptures; and I do not doubt that, when a future revision is undertaken, most of them will be adopted.

One of them was the omission of "*for*" before infinitives. The English Revisers declined to adopt this emendation; consequently we are favoured with such inconsistencies as the following:—

"*For* to go". Gen. xxxi. 18.
  See Ruth i. 18; "*to go*".
"*For* to come". Isa. xli. 22.
  See Jer. xl. 4; "*to come*".
"*For* to buy". Gen. xli. 57.
  See Gen. xlii. 7; "*to buy*".
"*For* to shew". Ex. ix. 16.
  See Neh. ix. 19; "*to shew*".
"*For* to gather". Ex. xvi. 27.
  See 2 Kings iv. 39; "*to gather*".

"*For* to deliver". Deut. xxv. 11.
    See Psa. xxxiii. 19; " to deliver ".

" *For* to give ". Deut. xxvi. 3.
    See Ex. xiii. 21; " *to give* ".

"*For* to keep". Josh. x. 18.
    See Gen. ii. 15; " *to keep* ".

" *For* to confirm". Ruth iv. 7.
    See 2 Kings xv. 19; " *to confirm* ".

" *For* to make". 1 Sam. i. 6.
    See Gen. iii. 6; " *to make* ".

" *For* to build". 1 Kings ix. 15.
    See Jer. xviii. 9; " *to build* ".

" *For* to search". 1 Chron. xix. 3.
    See Josh. ii. 2; " *to search* ".

"*For* to shed". Jer. xxii. 17.
    See Prov. i. 16; " *to shed* ".

" *For* to draw". Hag. ii. 16.
    See Gen. xxiv. 11; " *to draw* ".

" *For* to do ". Deut. iv. 1.
    See 2 Chron. ix. 8; " *to do* ".

In the Authorised Version of Gen. xlvii. 4, we read,

" *For* to sojourn in the land are we come."

From this verse the Revisers have eliminated the word "*for*"; and, as far as I have observed, it is the only instance of their having made the correction, and why they made it, and only it, I cannot tell.

By-the-bye, did they, upon reconsidering the matter, regret the loss of their favourite little word, and resolve to make amends for it by finding it a place elsewhere? I see that they have inserted the word in Neh. ii. 10; where, in the Authorised Version, it is not found. We now read,

> "And when Sanballat the Horonite, and Tobiah the servant, the Ammonite, heard of it, it grieved them exceedingly, *for* that there was come a man to seek the welfare of the children of Israel."

In the Authorised Version, which the Revisers thought to improve, it reads thus,

> "it grieved them exceedingly that", &c.

I need not say which is correct.

Another preposition which the Revisers very frequently misuse is "*in*". They do not discriminate between it and its cognate "*into*'; yet these two words are not interchangeable, they are not synonyms. "*Into*" has an active meaning, "*in*" has a passive meaning. You put a thing *into* its place, and then it is *in* its place. The Revisers say, Gen. l. 26, that Joseph's body was

"put *in* a coffin in Egypt";

they should have said that it was

"put *into* a coffin in Egypt."

The Revisers evidently knew that this is the correct word to use in such sentences, for in Neh. ii. 12, they have corrected this very error, and say,

"Neither told I any man what my God put *into* my heart".

In the Authorised Version, it is

"what my God had put *in* my heart".

In 2 Chron. ix. 23, we read,

"All the kings of the earth sought the presence of Solomon, to hear his wisdom, which God had put *in* his heart."

It should be,

"which God had put *into* his heart";

as it is in Neh. ii. 12, and vii. 5, thus,

"And my God put *into* my heart to gather together the nobles".

Why have the Revisers made this distinction between God's act in respect to the wisdom of Solomon, and His act in respect to the resolve of Nehemiah? They cannot answer.

For other instances of "*in*" for "*into*", see Gen. xliii. 22; Num. xxiii. 5, 12, 16; Deut. xxiv. 1, 3; 1 Kings x. 24; Ezra vii. 27; Psa. xl. 3; Isa. lix. 21 (see li. 23); Jer. xxxvii. 15, 18 (see verse 4).

What is the meaning of the following differences?

"The Lord spake *unto* Moses and *to* Aaron." Lev. xi. 1; and xv. 1 (See xiii. 1).

"Behold, I give *unto* him my covenant of peace: and it shall be *unto* him, and *to* his seed." Num. xxv. 13.

"I will neither turn *unto* the right hand nor *to* the left." Deut. ii. 27.

"The Lord saw that the wickedness of man was great *in* the earth. ... And it repented the Lord that he had made man *on* the earth. ... And God said ... Every thing that is *in* the earth shall die." Gen. vi. 5, 6, 13, 17.

Here is an awkward sentence; more than one fourth of the words composing it are prepositions. It is from 1 Kings viii. 6;

"And the priests brought *in* the ark *of* the covenant *of* the Lord *unto* its place, *into* the oracle *of* the house, *to* the most holy place, even *under* the wings *of* the cherubim."

The proper choice of prepositions is confessedly difficult to a foreigner; but Englishmen ought not to find any difficulty in making the proper selection. Poor little "*of*" seems to be the "*fag*"; it is made to do the work of "*with*", and "*by*", and "*on*", as well as its own work.

In Ex. xii. 16, we read,

"No manner of work shall be done in them,

save that which every man must eat, that only may be done *of* you."

Of course, it should be,

"that only may be done *by* you".

In 2 Sam. iv. 8 we read,

"Behold the head of Ish-bosheth the son of Saul thine enemy, which sought thy life; and the Lord hath avenged my lord the king this day *of* Saul, and *of* his seed."

It should be,

"*avenged* . . . . *on* Saul, and *on* his seed."

See Jer. v. 9, 29; ix. 9; there we read,

"Shall not my soul be *avenged on* such a nation as this?"

Sometimes "*of*" is made to do needless work; as, for instance, in Isa. xlvii. 9;

"despite *of* the multitude of thy sorceries";

this should be either,

"*in spite of the* multitude",

or else,

"*despite the* multitude".

In Ezk. xxxix. 12 we read,

> "Seven months shall the house of Israel be burying *of* them":

it should be,

> "burying them", not "burying *of* them".

Again, in Psa. xix. 11, we have,

> "In keeping *of* them there is great reward".

The error has been corrected by the Revisers in Lev. ix. 22, where, in the Authorised Version, we read,

> "And Aaron .... came down from offering *of* the sin-offering."

In the Revised Version it is,

> "And Aaron .... came down from offering the sin-offering."

Why did the Revisers correct the latter passage, and leave the former passages uncorrected?

Sometimes "*of*" is wrongly omitted, as in Gen. iv. 22, where we read,

> "Tubal-Cain, the forger of every cutting instrument of brass and iron."

It should be,

"every cutting instrument of brass and *of* iron";

otherwise, the statement means that the instruments were of a compound of brass and iron, and not separately of brass and of iron.

These are little matters, but they all tend to show the limited extent of the Revisers' knowledge of English.

## CHAPTER IX.

Contents.—Wiser than the wisest; Queen Esther not a woman; Moses not a man; Israel not a nation; omission of 'other'; 'none but'; 'other' redundant; 'none other', and 'no other'; 'beside', and besides'.

Is it not grotesquely absurd to state of one man that he was wiser than he was wise; and of another, that he was more brutish than he was brutish; and of one woman, that she was blessed more than she was blessed; and of another, that she was loved more than she was loved; and so on, of beasts, and nations, and peoples? Yet that is only what the Revisers have done. Turn to 1 Kings iv. 30, 31, and you will read,

> "Solomon's wisdom excelled the wisdom of all the children of the east, and all the wisdom of Egypt. For he was wiser than all men."

As the phrase "*all men*" must include Solomon, the statement is that he was wiser than himself, which is absurdly untrue.

The Revisers should have said,

> "He was wiser than all *other* men";

not "wiser than *all men*"; unless they meant to imply that he was either angelic or divine; and his life was not such as would lead us to draw *that* inference from it.

In Esther ii. 17, we read,

> "And the king loved Esther above all the women, and she obtained grace and favour in his sight more than all the virgins."

Was Esther, then, not a woman? And if not, what was she? Her name means "*secret*"; perhaps her nature also was secret.

What did the Revisers intend to assert about Moses when in Num. xii. 3 they said,

> "Now the man Moses was very meek, above all the men which were upon the face of the earth."

Was Moses not a man? Was he not upon

the face of the earth? In what sense, then, could he be said to be meeker than himself?

In Deut. xxviii. 1, we read,

> "It shall come to pass, if thou shalt hearken diligently unto the voice of the Lord thy God, . . . . that the Lord thy God will set thee on high above all the nations of the earth.'

The Jews were one of the nations of the earth; were they, then, to be set on high above themselves? If so, how?

The same error occurs in Psa. cxlvii. 20. See also Deut. x. 15; xiv. 2; and Esther iii. 8.

In 2 Chron. xi. 21, we read,

> "And Rehoboam loved Maacah the daughter of Absolom above all his wives and his concubines."

If, then, Maacah was neither Rehoboam's wife, nor one of his concubines, what was she?

In verses 18 and 20, it says,

> "And Rehoboam took him a wife, Mahalath, the daughter of Jerimoth the son of

David .... And after her he took him Maacah the daughter of Absolom".

Clearly she also was his wife; yet it is said that he loved her above all his wives. So he loved her more than he loved her! At least, that is what the Revisers say; but how he did it, they do *not* say.

In Jer. xvii. 9, we read,

"The heart is deceitful above all things".

But surely the expression "*all things*" must include the heart. Will the Revisers condescend to explain what they mean?

What meaning did the Revisers put, or expect us to put, on the words of Agur the son of Jakeh, which, in Prov. xxx. 2, are quoted thus,

"Surely, I am more brutish than any man"?

Who was Agur? It is evident that, though he was the son of Jakeh, he was not a man; for, the Revisers say that he was more brutish than any man. Perhaps he was a brute; but if so, why speak of his brutish nature? *cela va*

K

*sans dire.* And how came he to possess the faculty of speech? The Revisers have made a pretty puzzle of it.

Of course, the fault in each of these quotations is the omission of the word " *other* ",—

" more brutish than any *other* man ", &c.

In considering the word "*other*", the omission of it is not the only fault which has to be noticed: there is its very opposite,—its needless insertion.

In Gen. viii. 10, we read,

" Noah stayed yet *other* seven days; and again he sent forth the dove out of the ark."

Why "*other* seven days"? There had been no mention of a previous " *seven days* ".

The word " *other* " is redundant in Gen. xxviii. 17, also. There we read,

" How dreadful is this place! this is none *other* but the house of God, and this is the gate of heaven."

It should be either,

" this is *none but* the house of God ",

or else,

> "this is *none other than* the house of God".

The word *"other"* is redundant in Dan. ii. 11, likewise. There we read,

> "It is a rare thing that the king requireth, and there is none *other* that can shew it before the king, *except* the gods, whose dwelling is not with flesh."

It should be *"none...but"*, or *"none...other than"*, or *"none...except"*,

> "there is *none* that can shew it before the king, *except* the gods".

Let me ask also, why have we, in 1 Chron. xxiii. 17,

> "none other";

and in 1 Sam. xxi. 9,

> "no other"?

Can the Revisers give any reasons for this change? I trow not.

The latter passage is as follows,

> "And the priest said, The sword of Goliath

the Philistine, whom thou slewest in the vale of Elah, behold, it is here wrapped in a cloth behind the ephod: if thou wilt take that, take it; for there is *no other save that* here."

It should be, "there is no other", or "*none other than* that", or "there is *none save* that", or "there is *none besides* that".

This word "*besides*" reminds me of an oft-repeated error in the Revised Version. The words "*besides*" and "*beside*" are frequently misused there, one for the other.

They are of common origin, but have different and distinct meanings: "*beside*" means "by the side of", and therefore "in addition to"; but "*besides*" means "in addition to", but not necessarily "by the side of".

If this distinction be not observed, very awkward mistakes of meaning may be made; and the Revisers were quite aware of this, as is evident by their having corrected Num. v. 20.

In the Authorised Version the passage reads thus

ECCLESIASTICAL ENGLISH. 133

"But if thou hast gone aside to another instead of thy husband, and if thou be defiled, and some man have lain with thee *beside* thine husband".

The Revisers saw that this wording could but refer to three in a bed; and, conceiving that that is not the meaning of the original, they altered "*beside*" to "*besides*".

Additional evidence that they knew the proper meaning of "*beside*" is found in Neh. iii. 23. There in the Authorised Version we read,

"After him repaired Benjamin and Hashub, over against their house. After him repaired Azariah, the son of Maaseiah, the son of Ananiah, *by* his house."

This the Revisers have altered to

"*beside* his own house";

i.e., Azariah repaired that part of the wall of Jerusalem which was *by the side* of his own house. Had the Revisers said that he repaired the wall "*besides*" his own house, the meaning would have been that he repaired the wall *in addition* to repairing his own house. It is evident, then, that the Revisers clearly understood the distinctive meaning of each of the two words.

Is further evidence of this wanted? Then turn to Lev. ix. 17, where, in the Authorised Version we read,

> "He burnt it upon the altar, *beside* the burnt sacrifice of the morning."

Knowing that these words mean that the two offerings were burnt *side by side*, the Revisers substituted "*besides*" for "*beside*", to show that the statement intended to be made was that the one offering was supplementary to the other, and not necessarily coexistent with it. A similar correction is made in Num. xvi. 49. The word "*beside*" is used correctly in Lev. x. 12; xxv. 47; Num. vi. 9; Deut. xi. 30; xvi. 21; Josh. xii. 9; Ruth ii. 14; and the word "*besides*" is used correctly in Gen. xix. 12,

> "Hast thou here any *besides*?"

and in 2 Chron. xviii. 6,

> "Is there not here *besides* a prophet of the Lord?"

Now, why do I adduce these passages in proof of the Revisers' knowledge of the meaning of these two words? Simply to show how strangely the Revisers have utterly repudiated the teaching of their own lessons; as will be seen in the passages which I have to bring forward.

Turn now to 1 Sam ii. 2; 2 Sam. vii. 22; Isa. xliii. 11; xliv. 6, 8; and xlv. 6. All these passages refer to the oneness of the Deity; and, in every instance, the prepositional, instead of the adverbial, form of the word has been used.

So also is it in Gen. xxvi. 1; xxxi. 50; Lev. xxiii. 38, four times (compare ix. 17); and in Num. xxviii. 10, 15, 24, and 31; xxix. eleven times; also in Deut. xviii. 8; 2 Chron. xvii. 19, and elsewhere.

In my school days, if any boy had done this, and it could be proved that he knew better, he would have been called up *beside* the master; and, *besides* receiving a reproof, would have received something that would have made him almost *beside* himself with pain. I am speaking of more than fifty years ago. School discipline has much changed since then; and, apparently, so has the appreciation of pure English; for, the senior scholars (decidedly senior) who wilfully committed the errors which I have pointed out have received not even a gentle reproof for their errors, but have received instead, the thanks of Convocation. Poor Lindley Murray; *requiescat in pace!*

# CHAPTER X.

CONTENTS.—The Revisers' vacillation; 'alway', and 'always'; 'afterward', and 'afterwards'; 'toward', and 'towards'; 'forward', and 'forwards'; 'backward', and 'backwards'; 'upward', and 'upwards'; 'downward', and downwards'; 'inward', and 'inwards'; 'outward', and 'outwards'; 'time past', and 'times past'; 'while', and 'whiles'; 'this twenty years', and 'these twenty years'; 'every'; 'every one'; 'either' for 'each'; 'each of them'; 'each one'; 'one half'; 'eat', and 'eat up'; 'swallowed up', and 'swallowed down'.

I cannot but pity the Revisers, they seem to have been so bewildered by the intricacies of their mother tongue. No man among them appears to have possessed a perfect knowledge of the language combined with so commanding an influence over his fellows as to ensure the accurate expression of their thoughts in forcible and graceful English.

This is evidenced by their vacillation respecting numerous words and phrases; various instances of which have been given, and many more remain to be recorded.

For example, in Deut. xi. 1, we have "*alway*"; and, in verse 12 of the same chapter, "*always*". What did the Revisers wish us to understand by this difference; and, if they had no wish respecting it, why did they make the difference? This is not the only passage where it is found.

"*Alway*" occurs in Ex. xxv. 30; Num. ix. 16; Deut. xi. 1; xxviii. 29; 2 Sam. ix. 10; Job vii. 16; and Prov. xxviii. 14.

"*Always*" is found in Deut. v. 29; vi. 24, xi. 12; xiv. 23; Psa. xvi. 8; ciii. 9; Prov. v. 19; viii. 30; Eccl. ix. 8; and Isa. lvii. 16.

Then we have "*afterward*" and "*afterwards*"; and one altered to the other without any assignable reason; as in Jer. xxxiv. 11, where "*afterward*" has been altered by the Revisers to "*afterwards*"; yet in Jer. xvi. 16, the Revisers have inserted the very word which they have struck out of chapter xxxiv. 11!

"*Afterward*" occurs in Deut. xvii. 7; Jer. xvi. 16; xlix. 6; and Ezk. xliii. 1.

"*Afterwards*" is found in Deut. xiii. 9; Job xviii. 2; Prov. xx. 17; and Jer. xxxiv. 11.

The difference is the more strange, because the Revisers invariably say, "*toward*", not "*towards*"; "*forward*" and "*backward*", not "*forwards*" or "*backwards*"; they always say "*upward*" and "*downward*", never "*upwards*" or "*downwards*"; always "*inward*" and "*outward*", never "*inwards*" or "*outwards*", except where "*inwards*" is used as a noun.

Would that this uniformity were judiciously extended throughout the Revisers' work. They have made "*afterwards*" an exception in this class of words, without any reasonable ground upon which to base the exception.

Look at Ex. xxi. 29, 36; Deut. xix. 4, 6; and 1 Chron. ix. 20; in these passages we have the expression,

"in *time* past";

but in 2 Sam. iii. 17, the expression is,

"in *times* past";

while in Deut. iv. 42 the latter expression has

been altered to the former; and as the Revisers must, of course, be consistently inconsistent through their work, they have, in 2 Sam. v. 2, and 1 Chron. xi. 2, done the very reverse— they have altered the former expression into the latter.

The Revisers first alter "in *times* past" into "in *time* past"; and then alter "in *time* past", into "in *times* past". Was ever such childishness seen in the work of "most potent, grave, and reverend seigniors"? The passage in 2 Sam. v. 2 (and in 1 Chron. xi. 2), is, in the Authorised Version,

"In *time* past, when Saul was king";

this the Revisers have altered to,

"In *times* past, when Saul was king".

Was Saul king more than once, that the Revisers must needs make this alteration? The Scriptures are silent respecting it; whence, then, have the Revisers their information on this matter? or have they presumed to be wise "above that which is written," 1 Cor. iv. 6, with the usual result spoken of in Rom. i. 22?

There is another word, of similar meaning, which the Revisers have treated in a similarly capricious manner: viz., the word "while."

In Dan. iv. 31, we read,

> "*While* the word was in the king's mouth, there fell a voice from heaven".

But in the same book, Dan. ix. 20, 21, it is

> "*Whiles* I was speaking . . . . yea, *whiles* I was speaking".

"*Whiles*" occurs also in Ezk. xxi. 29; xliv. 17; and Hosea vii. 6.

Elsewhere, throughout the Old Testament, it is "*while*", not "*whiles*". See Deut. xxxi. 27; 1 Sam. xx. 14; 2 Sam. xii. 18, 21, 22; 1 Kings i. 14; 2 Chron. xv. 2; xxxiv. 3; Job xx. 23; Psa. vii. 2; xlix. 18; lxiii. 4; civ. 33; Isa. lv. 6; Jer. xv. 9; and xl. 5.

The Revisers' notions of singular and plural, though plural, are truly singular.

Turn to Gen. xxxi. 38; there you will read,

> "*This* twenty years have I been with thee".

Now look three verses lower down, and you will read,

> "*These* twenty years have I been in thy house".

Really, were the book not the Holy Bible, such English as this, would render it unworthy of criticism. And it is because it is the Holy Bible, that one feels so indignant with the Revisers for having put its truths into language so atrociously and absurdly inaccurate.

Surely we ought to give to God our very best, and not think any labour too great to bestow upon our offering. "What saith the Scripture?" Rom. iv. 3. "I will show thee that which is noted in the Scripture of Truth." Dan. x. 21. It is this:—"Ye brought that which was torn, and the lame, and the sick; thus ye brought an offering: should I accept this of your hand? saith the Lord. *But cursed be the deceiver, which hath in his flock a male, and voweth, and sacrificeth unto the Lord a corrupt thing.*" Mal. i. 13, 14. "Out of all your gifts ye shall offer every heave-offering of the Lord, *of all the best thereof*, even the hallowed part thereof out of it." Num. xviii. 29.

Did not the Revisers know that " *every* " is singular? Certainly it seems as if they did, when they altered Gen. xxxii. 16, from

> " *every* drove by *themselves* "

to

> " *every* drove by *itself* ".

In Ezk. xxxiii. 20 also, they say,

> " O house of Israel, I will judge you *every one* after *his* ways ".

But in Jonah iii. 8, they waver; and evidently being uncertain, yet desirous to be correct at least once, they give both forms in one verse, and say,

> " Let them turn *every one* from *his* evil way, and from the violence that is in *their* hands."

In Ezk. xxii. 6, there is a strange confusion of singular and plural. The Revisers have endeavoured to correct the Authorised Version, but have only partially succeeded. They say,

> " *Every one* according to *his* power, *have* been ".

The following passages are altogether wrong.

> "They did not *every man* cast away the abomination of *their* eyes". Ezk. xx. 8.
>
> "*Every man* to *your* tents, O Israel." 2 Chron. x. 16.
>
> "And so they set forward, *every man* by *their* families". Num. ii. 34.
>
> "These cities were *every one* with *their* suburbs round about *them*." Josh. xxi. 42.
>
> "They were *every one* of them head of *their* fathers' houses". Josh. xxii. 14.

Contrast the next two quotations.

> "They walked *every one* in the stubbornness of *their* evil heart." Jer. xi. 8.
>
> "Behold, ye walk *every one* after the stubbornness of *his* evil heart." Jer. xvi. 12.

What is to be said of the perpetrators of such inconsistencies as these in the Sacred Oracles? I can say only that I am sorry they are Englishmen.

Turn now to 2 Chron. xviii. 9. In the Authorised Version the passage reads thus,

> "The king of Israel, and Jehoshaphat king of Judah, sat *either of them* on his throne".

This, very properly, the Revisers have altered to,

> "The king of Israel and Jehoshaphat the king of Judah sat *each* on his throne".

The reason for this change is that "*either*" means one of two, but not both; and the passage, as it stood, meant that only one of them "*either*" the king of Israel *or* the king of Judah, "sat on *his* throne"; and this is not the meaning of the Hebrew.

Now, but for indisputable evidence, would it be believed that, within five pages of this correction, the Revisers have committed the very error which their own alteration of 2 Chron. xviii. 9 has condemned? Refer to 2 Chron. ix. 18, and to the corresponding passage in 1 Kings x. 19; the Authorised Version of the passage reads correctly thus,

> "There were six steps to the throne, with a footstool of gold, which were fastened to the throne, and stays on *each* side".

This the Revisers have "*revised*" thus,

L

> "There were six steps to the throne, with a footstool of gold, which were fastened to the throne, and stays on *either* side".

In the former passage the Revisers made right what was wrong; and in the latter they make wrong what was right; and they leave both passages as altered, to bear witness to their inexplicable inconsistency. It everywhere characterizes their work.

The Revisers have attempted to correct Lev. x. 1.

The passage, in the Authorised Version, reads thus,

> "And Nadab and Abihu, the sons of Aaron, took *either of them* his censer, and put fire therein."

This the Revisers have altered to "*each of them*".

I have spoken, on page 87, of the error of saying "*of them*" when all are meant; and the Revisers, in correcting 2 Chron. xviii. 9, very properly struck out those words; and, instead of saying

"sat *either of them* on his throne";
said
"sat *each* on his throne".

Yet, with the Revisers' peculiar consistency, they left the words "*of them*" when correcting Lev. x. 1, so that

"took *either of them* his censer",
is altered to,

"took *each of them* his censer".

As there were but two, it should be

"took *each* his censer".

It will be seen, then, that no dependence whatever can be placed on the finality of any correction made by the Revisers. Their vacillation is ceaseless, so that it is impossible to be heartily thankful for any wise correction made by them in any one place, without having ever present in our minds the feeling that in all probability we shall have to retract our thankful words before many more pages are read.

The following instances of redundancy must not pass without remark.

> "So Hanun took David's servants, and shaved off the *one* half of their beards." 2 Sam. x. 4.

Why did the Revisers say "*one* half"? Could there have been more halves than one, without there being the whole? It is sufficient to say "*half*". The expression, "*one* half", is pleonastic. So also is the word "*one*" in the following passages.

> "Each *one* had six wings." Isa. vi. 2.
> "Each *one* for his fathers' house." Num. i. 44.
> "Each *one* resembled the children of a king." Judges viii. 18.
> "Each *one* that walketh in his uprightness." Isa. lvii. 2.

In all these instances the word "*one*" is redundant; as the word "*each*" implies "oneness."

Can any person tell me what there is distinctively different in a moth's and a worm's manner of feeding, so that one must be said to "eat *up*" a thing, and the other simply to "eat" it? Look at Isa. li. 8;

"The moth shall *eat them up* like a garment,
and the worm shall *eat them* like wool."

What also is the difference which the Revisers intended us to understand between the expressions "swallowing *up*" and "swallowing *down*"? In Prov. xxi. 20, we read,

"There is [are] precious treasure and oil in the dwelling of the wise;
But a foolish man *swalloweth it up.*"

But in Job xx. 15, we are told,

"He hath *swallowed down* riches".

See also verse 18,

"That which he laboured for shall he restore, and shall not *swallow it down*".

The only other instance of the occurrence of the expression "swallow down" that I can recall to mind is in Job. vii. 19;

"How long wilt thou not look away from me,
"Nor let me alone till I *swallow down* my spittle?"

In other instances it is "*swallow up*"; though

what the Revisers intended by the difference, I must ask them to explain.

In Num. xvi. 32, 33 it says that,

> "The earth opened her mouth, and swallowed them *up*, .... and they went *down* alive into the pit."

Why did the Revisers say "swallowed them *up*"? There is some sense in speaking of a thing as being swallowed *down;* but "swallowed *up*" is not in accordance with the action of swallowing. Besides, it is sufficient to say, "*swallowed*",

> "The earth opened her mouth and swallowed them alive."

## CHAPTER XI.

CONTENTS.—'So—as', for 'as—as'; 'whether or no', for 'whether or not'; 'or', and 'nor'; 'not—or', and 'not—nor'; 'after' = 'according to'; 'never', and 'ever'; ambiguity of pronouns.

There are many other errors in the Revised Version of the Old Testament; some are the same as those which were committed by the Revisers of the New Testament, and have been commented on in '*The Revisers' English*', and therefore need but a passing remark here; others are new, and might be enlarged on; but I shall epitomize them all, for I am sure that my readers must be heartily tired of the subject.

"*So*—as", for "*as*—as", is a very common error. The rule respecting this matter will be found in '*The Revisers' English*', p. 141 of the 2nd edition. Evidently the Revisers of the Old Testament knew as little about it

## 152  ECCLESIASTICAL ENGLISH.

as did the Revisers of the New; for, where it was correct in the Authorised Version of the Old Testament, it has been "*revised*" [!] and made incorrect; e.g., in the Authorised Version of Psa. lxxii. 5, we read,

> "They shall fear thee *as* long *as* the sun and moon endure, throughout all generations."

This, in the Revised Version, has been altered to,

> "They shall fear thee while the sun endureth, And *so* long *as* the moon, throughout all generations."

Besides noticing the error of "*so* long as", for "*as* long as", look at the structure of the sentence, as *revised*. "They shall fear thee while the sun endureth, and so long as the moon, throughout all generations." "So long as the moon", what? The sentence is incomplete, and the meaning unintelligible; but, in the Authorised Version, all is clear.

Look at Gen. xliii. 34, and following verse. In the former we have the expression "*so* much as"; and, in the latter, "*as* much as". Yet both expressions are affirmative, and therefore both should have been "*as* much as".

In Lev. xxvi. 34, 35; Num. ix. 18, and Eccl. ii. 13, we have "*as—as*" used correctly. In all these passages the Revisers had the Authorised Version to guide them; the last passage reads thus,

> "Wisdom excelleth folly, *as* far *as* light excelleth darkness."

But in the very next chapter, viz. Eccl. iii. 12, where they were left to their own wisdom, they erred, saying,

> "There is nothing better for them, than to rejoice, and to do good *so* long *as* they live."

It should be,

> "*as* long *as* they live."

The same error occurs in Ex. xxx. 23; Deut. i. 11; 1 Sam. xxv. 22; xxix. 8; 1 Chron. xxi. 3; Esther v. 13; Job. xxvii. 6; and Prov. xxv. 16.

In Deut. ii. 5, *so—as* is correct, the statement being negative:

"I will not give you of their land, no, *not so much as* for the sole of your foot to tread on."

The mention of a negative statement reminds me of another error into which the Revisers have fallen, and consciously fallen; for it is an error which they have corrected elsewhere.

In Gen. xxxvii. 32, we read, in the Authorised Version,

" Know now whether it be thy son's coat or *no* ".

i.e.,

" Know now whether it *is* thy son's coat, or *no his coat* ".

The Revisers have corrected the " *no* " into " *not* "; but have left the " *be* ", which ought to have been " *is* ".

Again I have to ask, the oft-repeated question, Why have the Revisers corrected an error in one place, and left the very same error uncorrected in other places? Were the Revisers really in doubt as to which is the correct form? It seems so, for in Ex. xvi. 4, they write,

> "That I may prove them, whether they will walk in my law, or *no*."

i.e., "or *no* walk in it".

Compare the foregoing with Gen. xxvii. 21, where we have the correct form;

> "That I may feel thee, my son, whether thou be my very son Esau or *not*."

i.e., "or *not* my very son Esau."

Then in Deut. viii. 2, we have,

> "Whether thou wouldest keep his commandments, or *no*."

i.e., "or *no* keep them".

The Revisers, then, by way of maintaining their character for their peculiar consistency, once more give us the correct form. See Ex. xvii. 7,

> "Is the Lord among us, or *not?*"

See also Judges ii. 22.

Can an affirmative mean the same as a negative? The Revisers seem to think so; for, in Deut. xvii. 11, they say,

> "Thou shalt *not* turn aside .... to the right hand, *nor* to the left".

and in verse 20 of the same chapter, they say,

> "That he turn *not* aside .... to the right hand, *or* to the left."

In Num. xx. 17; Deut. xvii. 11; 2 Sam. ii. 19; and Prov. iv. 27, it is

> "*not* to the right hand, *nor* to the left";

but in Deut. v. 32; xvii. 20; xxviii. 14; Josh. i. 7; xxiii. 6; 1 Sam. vi. 12, and 2 Kings xxii. 2, it is

> "*not* to the right hand, *or* to the left".

What did the Revisers mean us to understand by this difference?

In the following passages also, we have "*not*" followed by "*nor*"; Ex. xii. 9; Deut. xxxi. 6; Josh. i. 6; Judges xiv. 16; Isa. xi. 9; xxxiv. 10; lx. 11; and lxv. 25.

But in these passages we have "*not*" followed by "*or*". 2 Chron. xvi. 1; Psa. cxxxii. 4; and Dan. iv. 19.

In Josh. i. 6 it is,

"I will *not* fail thee, *nor* forsake thee";

and, in the very next verse,

"Turn *not* to the right hand *or* to the left".

While speaking of "*not*", I must call attention to a passage in Psa. ciii.; there, in verse 10 in the Authorised Version, we read,

"He hath not dealt with us after our sins, nor rewarded us according to our iniquities."

In the Church Litany this passage is turned into a prayer, thus,

"O Lord, deal *not* with us *after* our sins, Neither reward us *after* our iniquities".

I well remember when a boy, refusing to say that prayer, and mentally saying, what I thought was the very reverse of it,

"O Lord *do* deal with us *after* our sins".

I thought it so awful to ask God not to have

anything to do with us *after* we had sinned; and it was not until I found the words in the ciii. Psalm, that I discovered, by the latter part of the passage, that "*after*" meant there, "*according to*". Thenceforth my trouble was at an end, and I always said,

> "O Lord, deal not with us *according to* our sins.
> Neither reward us *according to* our iniquities."

Judge then of my disappointment when, in the Revised Version, I found that the explanatory phrase "*according to*" had been struck out, and the ambiguous word, "*after*", had been repeated in the latter clause of the passage. It now reads thus,

> "He hath not dealt with us *after* our sins,
> Nor rewarded us *after* our iniquities."

Thanks be to God, that this passage as I used to understand it, and as, doubtless, many others have understood it, is not true. He does deal with us *after*, though in mercy not *according to*, our sins.

In 2 Chron. vi. 14, in the Authorised Version, we read,

> "There is no god like thee in the heaven, *nor* in the earth".

This, the Revisers wisely have altered to,

> "There is no God like thee, in the heaven, *or* in the earth".

So far, so good; but why leave other similar passages unaltered? In view of the foregoing alteration, we may reasonably ask, Why have we to read, in Deut. xiv. 27, 29; xviii. 1;

> "He hath no portion *nor* inheritance"?

In Judges xiii. 4, 7, we have,

> "Drink no wine *nor* strong drink";

and in Isa. liii. 2,

> "He hath no form *nor* comeliness";

and in Dan. ii. 10,

> "No king, lord, *nor* ruler, hath asked such a thing".

Again, in Dan. vi. 15,

> "No interdict *nor* statute which the king establisheth may be changed."

In all these passages it should be either
"no—*or*", or else "no—*nor any*". e.g.,

" No interdict *or* statute " ;

or else,

" No interdict, *nor any* statute ".

In Ex. xxiii. 26, we read,

"There shall none cast her young, *nor* be barren ",

and in Psa. xlix. 7,

" None *of them* can by any means redeem his brother,
*Nor* give to God a ransom for him."

These passages should be,

"There shall none cast her young, *or* be barren " ;

and,

" None can by any means redeem his brother,
*Or* give to God a ransom for him."

Why have the Revisers inserted the words "*of them*" in the last passage? There is nothing in the Hebrew to justify it; and the words do harm, for they make the passage imply that the impossibility of redeeming a soul, or of giving to God a ransom for him, is affirmed only "*of them*" of whom the Psalmist had just been speaking; whereas, if the words be not inserted, the statement is that "*none*" can do it.

Another question which I have to ask is, Why do the Revisers say "*never*", when they mean "*ever*"? In Gen. xxxiv. 12, we read,

> "Ask me *never* so much dowry and gift, and I will give according as ye shall say unto me".

In Job ix. 30, we read,

> "If I wash myself in snow water,
> And make my hands *never* so clean".

And in Psa. lviii. 5, we read,

> "They are like the deaf adder that stoppeth her ear;
> Which hearkeneth not to the voice of charmers,
> Charming *never* so wisely."

In each of these instances, "*never*" should be "*ever*"; the meaning being, "*to the extreme limit"*—as far as *ever* it is possible to go. "*Never*" is, of course, the exact opposite.

It is very odd that the Revisers should, against their will, state what they so plainly do not mean, and should obscurely state what they so plainly mean. For instance, Gen. iv. 17, says,

> "And Cain knew his wife; and she conceived, and bore Enoch: and he [who?] builded a city, and called the name of the city, after the name of his son, Enoch."

It is not until we have read to the end of the verse that we find out that "*he*" does not refer to Enoch, as it seems to do, but to Cain.

Again, in Gen. ii. 21, we read,

> "The Lord God caused a deep sleep to fall upon the man, and he slept; and he [who, the man?] took one of his ribs, and closed up the flesh instead thereof."

But for our well-knowing the circumstance, we might have imagined, from the wording of this verse, the absurdity that the man took out one of his own ribs.

I would suggest that in a re-revision of the Scriptures, the personal pronoun, when referring to the Deity, be printed in capitals. Then this passage will be,

> "The Lord God caused a deep sleep to fall upon the man, and he slept; and HE took one of his ribs".

Turn now to 2 Kings xxiii. 29, and without reading the next verse, decide, if you can, who was the slayer, and who was the slain.

> "In his days, Pharaoh-necoh king of Egypt went up against the king of Assyria to the river Euphrates: and king Josiah went against him; and *he* slew *him* at Megiddo, when *he* had seen *him*."

This is nearly as lucid as was the evidence given by a witness in a case of manslaughter in Somersetshire,

> "*He'd* a stick, and *he'd* a stick; and *he* licked *he*, and *he* licked *he*; and if *he'd* a-licked *he*, as hard as *he* licked *he*, *he'd* a-killed *he*, and not *he, he*."

# CHAPTER XII.

CONTENTS.—Pronouns; 'who', and 'which'; 'ye', and 'you'; 'his', and 'your'; 'they', and 'your'; 'your', and 'thy'; 'turn ye', and 'turn you'; 'thou', and 'thee'; 'in them', and 'in those'; 'his', and 'it'; 'the man's rod whom'; 'John Smith, his book'; 'beside', and 'besides'; 'again'.

The Revisers' errors in the use of pronouns are very numerous. By "*The Revisers*", I mean always the English Revision Company; for, many of the errors were protested against by the American Revision Company, but protested against in vain. One of those errors was the use of "*which*", applied to persons. It will be seen in the Appendix to the Revised Version of the Scriptures that the Americans wished to substitute "*who*", or "*that*", for "*which*", when applied to persons. Had that been done, we should have been spared such inconsistencies as the following;

## ECCLESIASTICAL ENGLISH. 165

"The man of God, *who*". 1 Kings xiii. 26.

"Obadiah, *which*". 1 Kings xviii. 3.

"The son of Shaphat, *who*". 1 Kings xix. 19.

"The son of Hilkiah, *which*". 2 Kings xviii. 18, 37.

"O Lord, the God of Israel, . . . . . *who*". 2 Chron. vi. 14. 15.

"The Lord, the God of their fathers, *which*". 2 Chron. vii. 22.

"The Lord thy God, *which* brought thee forth". Deut. viii. 14.

"The Lord thy God, *who* brought thee forth". Deut. viii. 15.

As the English Revisers refused to comply with the wish of their American friends for uniformity in this matter, they have a right to know why "*which*" was altered to "*who*" in 2 Chron. vi. 15; 1 Sam. xii. 8; and Psa. cxxxv. 21; and why, *remembering these alterations*, it was not altered in Job v. 9; Psa. vii. 10; Isa. xxviii. 29; and other passages.

Let me also ask why we have, in Psa. cxxiv. 8,

"Our help is in the name of the Lord *who* made heaven and earth";

and in Psa. cxlvi. 5, 6, 7,

"Happy is he that hath the God of Jacob for his help,
*Which* made heaven and earth;
*Which* keepeth truth for ever;
*Which* executeth judgement for the oppressed;
*Which* giveth food to the hungry."

and then, in the very next Psalm, verses 7 and 8,

"Sing praises upon the harp unto our God;
*Who* covereth the heaven with clouds,
*Who* prepareth rain for the earth,
*Who* maketh grass to grow upon the mountains."

Here are other instances of the Revisers' inconsistency. Josh. xxiv. 13, is as follows,

"I gave *you* a land whereon *thou* hadst not laboured, and cities which *ye* built not".

Here "*you*" and "*ye*" are right; but why has the singular pronoun "*thou*" been inserted in the middle of the sentence? Why change from plural to singular, and then from singular to plural, all in one verse?

In Zech. vii. 10, we have,

> "Let none of you imagine evil against *his* brother in *your* heart."

Probably the Revisers thought that if they had said "*his* heart" the pronoun would have referred to "*brother*". But why did they not transpose the latter part of the sentence and say,

> "Let none of you imagine evil in *his* heart against *his* brother"?

See also Zech. viii. 17. In Ex. xxx. 15, we have,

> "The rich shall not give more, and the poor shall not give less, than the half shekel, when *they* give the offering of the Lord, to make atonement for *your* souls."

It should be,

> "when *they* give the offering of the Lord, to make atonement for *their* souls."

In Lev. xxiii. 22, a similiar confusion of pronouns occurs.

> "When *ye* reap the harvest of *your* land, *thou* shalt not wholly reap the corners of *thy* field, neither shalt *thou* gather the gleaning of *thy* harvest: *thou* shalt leave them for the poor".

See also Deut. vii. 4,

> "So will the anger of the Lord be kindled against *you*, and he will destroy *thee* quickly."

In Deut. xxix. 5, we have,

> "*Your* clothes are not waxen old upon *you*, and *thy* shoe is not waxen old upon *thy* foot."

Then in verse 11 of the same chapter, we have,

> "*Your* little ones, *your* wives, and *thy* stranger that is in the midst of *thy* camps, from the hewer of *thy* wood unto the drawer of *thy* water."

But why multiply examples of this error? They abound in the Revisers' work.

However, I must give one more; it is really too good to be omitted. See 2 Sam. vii. 23. I will quote part of the previous verse in order to make the reference of the pronouns plain—if possible.

> "There is none like *thee*, neither is there any God beside [besides] *thee*, according to all that we have heard with our ears. And what one nation in the earth is like *thy* people, even like Israel, whom *God* went to redeem unto *himself* for a people, and to make *him* a name, and to do great things for *you*, and terrible things for *thy* land, before *thy* people, which *thou* redeemedst to *thee* out of Egypt"?

Here we have first, God addressed in the second person, "*thee*" and "*thy*"; then He is spoken of in the third person as "*God*", and "*himself*", and "*him*"; then, without any indication that the speaker is addressing any one else, we have "*you*", which appears to refer to the Israelites; then another change, again without any indication of change of person addressed, and we have "*thy*", "*thy*", "*thou*", and "*thee*", in the second person, though the reference is to God, who just before has been spoken of in the third person, as "*himself*", and "*him*"!

Do the Revisers think that "ye" is singular? It appears so, for in Micah i. 11, they say,

> "Pass *ye* away, O inhabitant of Shaphir".

In Isa. xxxi. 6, we read,

> "Turn *ye* unto him from whom *ye* have deeply revolted";

and in Ezk. xxxiii. 11, we read,

> "Turn *ye*, turn *ye* from your evil ways";

but in Prov. i. 23, it is,

> "Turn *you*, at my reproof";

and in Zech. ix. 12, it is,

> "Turn *you* to the strong hold, *ye* prisoners of hope".

In Psa. xxv. 16, we read,

> "Turn *thee* unto me, and have mercy upon me",

but in Psa. lxix. 16, it is,

"According to the multitude of thy tender mercies turn *thou* unto me."

"*Thou*" is nominative, "*thee*" is accusative; therefore they are no more interchangeable than are "*I*" and "*me*". We may say,

"Turn *thyself* unto me";

or we may say,

"Turn *thou* unto me";

but we may not say,

"Turn *thee* unto me".

Members of the Society of Friends, for whom I have the greatest respect, frequently err in this matter.

The Revisers are evidently among those who are given to change, Prov. xxiv. 21; hence, in Ex. xxxv. 35, we have to read,

"*Of them* that do any workmanship, and *of those* that devise cunning works."

In Psa. cxlvii. 11, we read,

> "The Lord taketh pleasure *in them* that fear him.
>
> *In those* that hope in his mercy,"

and in Psa. lxix. 6, we read,

> "*Let not them* that wait on thee be ashamed:
>
> . . . . .
>
> *Let not those* that seek thee be brought to dishonour."

See also Ex. xxxv. 35.

The Revisers' errors in the use of pronouns are, as I have said, innumerable. I can give only examples of them. See how the singular and plural are mixed in the following passage. Deut. xxii. 1, 2,

> "Thou shalt not see thy brother's ox *or* his sheep go astray, and hide thyself from *them:* thou shalt surely bring *them* again unto thy brother. And if thy brother be not nigh unto thee, or if thou know him not, then thou shalt bring *it* home to thine house, and *it* shall be with thee until thy brother seek after *it*, and thou shalt restore *it* to him again."

Of course, the word "*again*" is redundant,

unless the reference is to an animal that had previously been restored to the loser; and that, the passage does not imply.

One more example. See Dan. iv. 14, 15,

> "He cried aloud, and said thus, Hew down the tree, and cut off *his* branches, shake off *his* leaves, and scatter *his* fruit: let the beasts get away from under *it*, and the fowls from *his* branches. Nevertheless leave the stump of *his* roots in the earth . . . . and let *it* be wet with the dew of heaven, and let *his* portion be with the beasts in the grass of the earth."

While speaking of pronouns, I would call attention to the Revisers' alteration of Num. xvii. 5. In the Authorised Version it is,

> "It shall come to pass, that *the man's rod, whom* I shall choose, shall blossom".

As I pointed out in a paper which I read before the Royal Society of Literature (upon common errors in speaking and writing), the expression, "*the man's rod, whom*", is very objectionable.

The Revisers saw the error, and tried to correct it, but how have they done it? Thus,

"It shall come to pass, that the man whom 1 shall choose, his rod shall bud";

which is as graceful a form of expression as is, "*John Smith, his book*".

Why did not the Revisers say,

"It shall come to pass that the rod, of the man whom I shall choose, shall bud"?

# CHAPTER XIII.

CONTENTS:—Positive assertions weakening; 'ever and ever'; 'from everlasting to everlasting'; 'shall', and 'will'; 'compass us round'; 'shall', for 'should'; 'lift', and 'lifted'; 'we be'; 'be surely', and 'surely be'; 'none was', and 'none were'; 'the distance were'; 'dwelt unto this day'; 'get thee to Anathoth'.

There are some forms of expression which we weaken by our very endeavours to strengthen them. For instance, if I say, "There were two thousand persons present", I make a statement which those who hear me, believe to be founded on trustworthy information. But, if I say, "*I am sure* there were two thousand persons present", it is at once understood that the number is doubtful; and, by my saying "*I am sure*, they know that I am *not* sure, but am only estimating the number of persons that were present.

These remarks apply to the expression, "*for*

*ever and ever*", which is repeatedly found in the Revisers' work, e.g., in Ex. xv. 18; 1 Chron. xxix. 10; Psa. ix. 5; x. 16; xxi. 4; xlv. 6, 17; xlviii. 14; lii. 8; cxix. 44; cxlv. 1, 2; cxlviii. 6; Isa. xxx. 8; xxxiv. 10; Dan. ii. 20; vii. 18; xii. 3; Micah iv. 5.

The mischief of the expression "for ever and ever", is that it most unmistakably implies that "*for ever*" does not mean "*eternally*"; for if it does, why add "*and ever*"? Besides, how can there be any extension of existence to that which is eternal? And if one "*for ever*" does not mean "*eternally*", how can two, or even two thousand, "*for evers*" mean it? No number of finites can make an infinite. Therefore, by endeavouring to strengthen the expression "*for ever*", by adding "*and ever*" to it, you utterly destroy its meaning.

In 1 Chron. xvi. 36; Neh. ix. 5; Jer. vii. 7, and xxv. 5, the Revisers have struck out the expression "*for ever and ever*", and have substituted for it, "from everlasting even to everlasting", "from everlasting to everlasting", "from of old even for evermore", and "from of old and even for evermore."

Of these four forms of expression, the two latter are the most to be preferred; because we can with propriety speak of some thing as existing *from* some *definite* past time onward for ever; but we cannot with propriety speak of anything as existing "*from* everlasting *to* everlasting"; because *from* one thing *to* another, implies that there is an interval between them, and that idea is inconsistent with the term "*everlasting*".

The Revisers' errors in the use of the auxiliaries "*shall*" and "*will*" are very strange. We are accustomed to find foreigners perplexed by them; but Englishmen should know their own language. However, it is clear that there are some who do not. The Revisers, of course, think that they do; hence, in Gen. xxxiv. 30, they have altered "*shall*" to "*will*", and, in so doing, were right. The verse reads thus in the Revised Version,—

"And Jacob said to Simeon and Levi, ye have

> troubled me, to make me to stink among the inhabitants of the land, among the Canaanites and the Perizzites: and, I being few in number, they *will* gather themselves together against me and smite me; and I shall be destroyed, I and my house."

The alteration was necessary because *"shall"*, in the third person, implies compulsion on the part of the speaker, whereas *"will"* implies futurity only; and that was what was intended by Jacob.

But why, seeing that the Revisers have made this judicious alteration, have they left unaltered numerous other similar passages? For instance, that in Joshua vii. 9, which is an almost parallel passage; why was it left? It is as follows:

> "Oh [O] Lord, what shall I say, after that Israel hath [*have*] turned *their* backs before their enemies! For the Canaanites and all the inhabitants of the land *shall* hear of it, and *shall* compass us round, and cut off our name from the earth".

This should be,

> "the inhabitants of the land *will* hear of it, and *will* compass us, and cut off our name from the earth".

There is no occasion to say "compass us *round*". The word "*round*" is comprehended in the word "*compass*".

In Gen. iv. 13, 14, we read,

> "And Cain said . . . . I shall be a fugitive and a wanderer in [*on*] the earth; and it *shall* come to pass that whosoever findeth me *shall* slay me."

Of course, the Revisers should have said,

> "it *will* come to pass, that whosoever findeth me *will* slay me." See also Gen. xii. 12.

In Num. xiv. 13, we read,

> "And Moses said unto the Lord, Then the Egyptians *shall* hear it".

This would have been all very well if Moses had been threatening to tell the Egyptians; but he was not; he was simply saying what *would* happen, not what *should* happen. The

Revisers therefore should have rendered his words thus,

"Then the Egyptians *will* hear it".

In 1. Sam. xix. 11, Michal, David's wife, warns him of her father's intention to kill him, and says, according to the Revisers' interpretation of her words,

"If thou save not thy life to-night, tomorrow thou *shalt* be slain."

It ought to be,

"tomorrow thou *wilt* be slain."

In Ezk. xiv. 16, 18, 20 we read of dire judgments being threatened by God against a land; and the certainty of the execution of those judgments is enforced by the utterance of these thrice repeated words,

"Though these three men [Noah, Daniel, and Job] were in it, as I live, saith the Lord God, they *shall* deliver neither sons nor daughters; they only *shall* be delivered".

As this is the *future* subjunctive, as shown by the verb "*were*", the sentence should be,

"Though these three men *were* in it, as I live, saith the Lord God, they *should* deliver neither sons nor daughters; they only *should* be delivered".

Errors of this kind abound throughout the work. See Deut. i. 39; 1 Sam. xix. 11; 1 Kings viii. 42; xii. 27; xviii. 12, 14; Neh. iv. 3; Esther i. 17, 20; ii. 11; Psa. lxxxv. 12, 13; cxxxix. 10; Isa. lvii. 16; Jer. xxvi. 15; and elsewhere.

In Psalm xxiii. 6, we have "*shall*" for "*will*", and "*will*" for "*shall*":

"Surely goodness and mercy *shall* follow me all the days of my life:
And I *will* dwell in the house of the Lord for ever."

It should be,

Surely goodness and mercy *will* follow me all the days of my life:
And I *shall* dwell in the house of the Lord for ever."

The reason of this is that "*shall*", in the third person, implies compulsion on the part of the speaker, whereas "*will*" implies futurity only, as I have previously explained; and "*will*", in the first person implies volition, whereas "*shall*" in the first person is simply indicative of futurity, without any reference to volition.

David did not say, " Goodness and mercy *shall* follow me "; that would have been equivalent to saying that he had the ordering of the providence of God; but he did say, " Goodness and mercy *will* follow me ", which is an expression of trust in God's loving-kindness. Neither did he say, "*I will* dwell in the house of the Lord for ever ". He knew very well that

> " 'Tis of grace from first to last,
> That sinners enter Heaven ";

and, trusting in God's grace, he said,

> " I *shall* dwell in the house of the Lord for ever."

The Revisers' language is the utterance of

proud presumption; David's language was the expression of child-like faith.

I have previously cited some instances of the Revisers' inconsistencies in the use of verbs, but "the half was not told". Here are some more.

"Hagar *lift* up her voice". Gen. xxi. 16.
"Abraham *lifted* up his eyes". Gen. xxii. 4.
"Abraham *lift* up his eyes". Gen. xviii. 2.
"Aaron *lifted* up his hands". Lev. ix. 22.
"We *are* twelve brethren". Gen. xlii. 13.
"We *be* twelve brethren". Gen. xlii. 32.
"If I *be* bereaved of my children,
I *am* bereaved". Gen. xliii. 14.
"I am the Lord *that* heal*eth* thee". Ex. xv. 26.
"I am the Lord *which* sancti*fy* you". Lev. xx. 8.
"He shall *be surely* put to death". Ex. xxi. 15.
"He shall *surely be* put to death". Ex. xxi. 16.
"*None were* of silver". 1 Kings x. 21.
"*None was* exempted". 1 Kings xv. 22.
"*Though it is* a forest". Josh. xvii. 18.
"*Though they be* strong". Josh. xvii. 18.
"Thou *hast been* a strong hold to the poor, a

strong hold to the needy in his distress, a refuge from the storm, a shadow from the heat, when the blast of the terrible ones *is* as a storm against the wall." Isa. xxv. 4.

The Revisers cannot justify this change in the verb, from the past to the present; for, the verb in the Hebrew is not written; it is understood; and is, of course, understood, in the latter clause, to agree with the time of the previous verb, i.e.,

> "Thou *hast been* a refuge . . . . when the blast *was* as a storm ".

Again,

> "From the uttermost part of the one wing unto the uttermost part of the other *were* ten cubits." 1 Kings vi. 24.

What *were?* The distance *were!* *Were* it? The verb is not expressed in the Hebrew; therefore, to the Revisers be all the glory of the grammar.

> "Art thou the man of God that cam*est* from Judah ?" 1 Kings xiii. 14.

In this verse the nominative to the verb

"*came*" is not the pronoun "*thou*", but "*the man of God*"; and we cannot say, "the man of God cam*est*." The meaning is,

> "Art thou — the man of God that came from Judah?"

Again, in the Revised Version, we read,

> "The children of Benjamin did not drive out the Jebusites that inhabited Jerusalem: but the Jebusites dwel*t* with the children of Benjamin in Jerusalem, *unto this day*." Judges i. 21.

This should have been,

> "the Jebusites *have dwelt* with the children of Benjamin in Jerusalem, *unto this day*."

In the Authorised Version it is "*dwell*". Even that is preferable to "*dwelt*".

"*Dwelt*" refers wholly to the past, and therefore cannot be used in connection with "*unto this day*". But "*have dwelt*" can be used in that connection; and, being so used, means,

> "have continued to dwell unto this day."

As has frequently been said, any error made in one direction in the Revisers' work, is almost certain to be accompanied by a corresponding error in the opposite direction. Hence, we are not surprised at the following:

Solomon said unto Abiathar the priest (1 Kings ii. 26),

> "Get thee [*thou*] to Anathoth, unto thine own fields; for thou art worthy of death: but I will not at this time put thee to death, because thou bar*est* the ark of the Lord God before David my father".

How could Abiathar bare the ark before one who was dead and buried? The verb should be in the past, to agree with the event; and the last clause of the verse should be transposed, so that the sense would not be dependent on a comma.

The passage should read thus,

> "Get *thou* to Anathoth, unto thine own fields, for thou art worthy of death; but, because thou bar*edst* the ark of the Lord God before David my father, I will not at this time put thee to death".

# CHAPTER XIV.

CONTENTS.—The Rule respecting verbs that are not expressed. 'I had rather be'; 'thence', and 'from thence'; 'whence', and 'from whence'; the natural place of emphasis.

The Revisers have corrected a very common error, which occurs in the Authorised Version of Prov. iii. 16. The nominative in the first part of the verse being in the singular, of course the verb also is in the singular to agree with it; and the nominative in the last part of the verse being in the plural, the verb also should be in the plural; but, being omitted, the verb in the first part of the verse is understood as applying to the last, but being in the singular, does not agree with it. The verse is as follows:

> "Length of days *is* in her right hand; and in her left hand [*is*] riches and honour."

This has been corrected thus,
> "Length of days *is* in her right hand:
> In her left hand *are* riches and honour."

Prov. xviii. 4, also has been corrected. In the Authorised Version it reads thus,
> "The words of a man's mouth *are* as deep waters, and the well-spring of wisdom [*are*] as a flowing brook."

This has been corrected thus,
> "The words of a man's mouth *are* as deep waters;
> The wellspring of wisdom *is* as a flowing brook."

Now, is it not strange that the Revisers, who by making the foregoing alterations showed that they understood the rule respecting such sentences, should have given us such sentences as the following?
> "Lord, my heart *is* not haughty nor [*is*] mine eyes lofty". Psa. cxxxi. 1.
> "God *is* in heaven, and thou [*is*] upon earth". Eccl. v. 2.
> "The vineyard of the Lord of hosts *is* the

house of Israel, and the men of Judah [*is*] his pleasant plant ". Isa. v. 7.

" The sword *is* without, and the pestilence and the famine [*is*] within ". Ezk. vii. 15.

" Whose leaves *were* fair, and the fruit thereof [*were*] much ". Dan. iv. 21.

" Behold a man clothed in linen, whose loins were girded with pure gold of Uphaz: his body also *was* like the beryl, and his face as the appearance of lightning, and his eyes [*was*] as lamps of fire, and his arms and his feet [*was*] like in colour to burnished brass, and the voice of his words [*was*] like the voice of a multitude." Dan. x. 5, 6.

It should be,

" Behold a man clothed in linen, whose loins *were* girded with pure gold of Uphaz : his body also *was* like the beryl, and his face as the appearance of lightning ; his eyes *were* as lamps of fire, and his arms and his feet like in colour to burnished brass ; and the voice of his words *was* like the voice of a multitude."

Where the number of the nominative changes,

the verb must be repeated and be made to agree with its nominative.

How is it that the Revisers fall into that common error of using "*had*" for "*would*"? They would never think of saying,

"I *had* be";

yet, in Psa. lxxxiv. 10, they say,

"I *had* rather be a doorkeeper".

Of course, it should be,

"I *would* rather be a doorkeeper".

The presence of the adverb "*rather*" cannot affect the verb; therefore, as it is wrong to say "I *had* be", it must be wrong to say "I *had* rather be".

In Obadiah 4, we read, in the Authorised Version,

"Though thou exalt *thyself* as the eagle, and though thou set thy nest among the stars, *thence* will I bring thee down, saith the Lord."

This is altered, in the Revised Version, thus,

"Though thou mount on high as the eagle,

and though thy nest be set among the stars, I will bring thee down *from thence*, saith the Lord."

The simile is drawn from the rock-dwellings of the Edomites; but the beauty and force of the old Version has been sadly marred by the Revisers.

'*The Vision of Obadiah*' had for its object the denouncing of the arrogancy [sic] of Edom; (see v. 3) and, bearing that in mind, the expression "*exalt thyself*" is certainly to be preferred to "*mount on high*", notwithstanding that the latter expression may be more suitable, in speaking of an eagle; for we ought not, in using symbolic language, to lose sight of the purport of the simile, but should judiciously blend the words suitable to each state, the real and the symbolic, as has been carefully done in this passage in the Authorised Version.

Further, the expression,

"though thy nest *be set* among the stars",

does not so graphically describe the arrogancy

of Edom, as does the expression in the Authorised Version,

"though *thou set* thy nest among the stars".

The passive form of the verb has less force than has the active. Also, the transposition of the last clause is bad, because it weakens the declaration

"I will bring thee down from thence, saith the Lord."

Far stronger is it as it stands in the Authorised Version,

"Thence will I bring thee down, saith the Lord."

The verse is divided into two parts; the former part, consisting of two clauses, relates to the proud bearing of the Edomites,

"Though thou exalt thyself as the eagle, and though thou set thy nest among the stars";

and the latter part relates to God's threatened debasement of the Edomites,

"Thence will I bring thee down, saith the Lord."

Now, as I have previously said, the natural places of emphasis in a sentence, or in a clause of a sentence, are those occupied by the first and the last words; the intermediate words occupy places of inferior emphasis.

The writers of the Authorised Version admirably illustrate this in the verse which is under consideration, especially in the last clause, the first and last words of which are "*thence*" and "*Lord*". Emphasize these words, and likewise the first and last words of the two previous clauses, and mark the power of the expression.

" *Though* thou exalt thyself as the *eagle*,
and
*Though* thou set thy nest among the *stars*,
*Thence* will I bring thee down, saith the *Lord*."

How feeble is the Revised Version of this!

" I will bring thee down from thence, saith the Lord."

However, I have not, in these criticisms, asked my readers to consider graces of style, and such like higher matters; that were a hopeless task with such writings as the Revisers' before us. It will be time enough to consider the higher branches of the study of the language of the Sacred Scriptures, when the Revisers have learnt to express themselves grammatically.

The primary object which I had in calling attention to Obadiah 4 was to criticize the Revisers' alteration of "*thence*" to "*from thence*"; an alteration which is certainly not for the better.

"*Thence*", "*hence*", and "*whence*" mean, respectively, "*from* there", "*from* here", and "*from* where"; they carry in themselves the meaning of "*from*"; consequently, to say "*from thence*", is equivalent to saying "*from from there*".

The absurdity of the Revisers' alteration is therefore apparent, though their motive in making it is certainly not so. I must concede that they had a motive; but what it was, it is impossible to even imagine, for, on the very same page where they have substituted "*from thence*" for "*thence*", they have five times employed the word "*thence*", in sentences strictly parallel with Obadiah 4. Here are the words; judge for yourselves. The passage containing them is Amos ix. 2—4.

> " Though they dig into hell, *thence* shall mine hand take them; and though they climb up to heaven, *thence* will I bring them down. And though they hide themselves in the top of Carmel, I will search and take them out *thence;* and though they be hid from my sight in the bottom of the sea, *thence* will I command the serpent, and he shall bite them. And though they go into captivity before their enemies, *thence* will I command the sword, and it shall slay them."

The passage in Obadiah is not the only one in which the Revisers have altered "*thence*" to "*from thence*"; they have made the same ridiculous alteration in 1 Chron. xiii. 6, and 2 Chron. viii. 18. But, with their usual inconsistency, they have left the word unaltered elsewhere. So we have,

"Abraham journeyed *from* *thence*". Gen. xx. 1.

"Isaac departed *thence*". Gen. xxvi. 17.

"Isaac removed *from thence*". Gen. xxvi. 22.

"The Lord thy God brought thee out *thence*". Deut. v. 15.

"He brought us out *from thence*". Deut. vi. 23.

Quite as faulty are the Revisers in their use of the adverbs "*hence*" and "*whence*". e.g.,

"Carry up my bones *from hence.*" Gen. l. 25.

"Carry up my bones away *hence.*" Ex. xiii. 19.

"Carry us not up *hence.*" Ex. xxxiii. 15.

"Get thee down quickly *from hence.*" Deut. ix. 12.

"*Whence* comest thou?" Job i. 7.

"*From whence* comest thou?" Job ii. 2.

"*Whence* come ye?" Gen. xlii. 7.

"*From whence* come ye?" Josh. ix. 8.

And so on, to the end of the Bible.

## CHAPTER XV.

CONTENTS.—'This', and 'that'; change of proper names; 'O', and 'oh'; 'wilt', and 'willest'; 'if' for 'whether'; 'though' for 'if'; 'except' for 'unless'; the first use of 'its'; 'nitre' for 'natron'; 'brass' for 'copper'; 'bits' for 'bridles'; 'Aha' for 'Ha, Ha'; roaring like a lion; youth like an eagle; 'people of his pasture'; 'sheep of his hand'; 'who was Sarai Abram?'; again the second time; 'sick of' and 'sick with'; heavier than them is!

Lord Iddesleigh, in his address to the students of the University of Edinburgh, said, "Some persons are so intent upon details that they lose all idea of the whole, and for want of grasp of the whole, they lose the benefit of the very details with which they so energetically busy themselves."

This remark is singularly applicable to the Revisers. Intent upon the jots and tittles of their work, they have failed to take a comprehensive view of the whole, with the object of bringing, as it were into the unity of brotherhood, the various forms of expression which, in their heterogeneous characters, must be considered as aliens to the commonwealth of our language.

However, let us hope that some day the work will be taken up again; and that then it will be in the hands of those who will have crowned their other qualifications by superadding a perfect knowledge of their own mother tongue.

There still remain certain errors to be criticized, but I will be very brief with them all, for I fear to tire my readers by dwelling on a subject which is universally held to be devoid of interest.

I grant that the study of English is uninteresting to most persons; but, had it been so to all, where would have been that powerful command of words which has so often held captive the minds of multitudes who have listened with entrancement to the overflowing eloquence of our orators; or where would have been the thrilling music of language heard in the rhythm of poetry?

Do my readers think that the orator and the poet have not to study their utterances? No man ever arrived at eminence in any art without much study. True, "*poeta nascitur, non fit*", but that refers to the constitution of the mind, not to poetic diction. The feelings and thoughts, which are the soul of poetry and eloquence, are given; but the command of language, adequate to express those feelings and thoughts, is the result of diligent study by a highly sensitive mind and keenly appreciative intellect.

But I must not linger over this engaging subject; I must descend from the sublime to the ridiculous; for my present duty is to call attention to errors, not to descant on the raptures of eloquence and poetry.

And truly my subject is ridiculous, for one cannot but laugh at the Revisers' absurd mistakes.

Are the words "*this*" and "*that*" interchangeable? Are nearness and distance one and the same thing? The Revisers say, in

2 Kings iii. 16, 17,

> "Make *this* valley full of trenches. For thus saith the Lord, Ye shall not see wind, neither shall ye see rain, yet *that* valley shall be filled with water."

What confusion the change of names makes in the Second Book of Kings! We read there, in chapter xi. verse 2, of *Joash*, the son of Ahaziah, king of Judah. But, in verse 21 of the same chapter, and in xii. 1, 2, 4, 6, 7, 18, and xiv. 13, he is called "*Jehoash*"; then, in xii. 19, 20, and xiii. 1, he is again called "*Joash*". This is the more confusing because the name of the king of *Israel*, who was cotemporary with Jehoash, the king of *Judah's* successor, was *Jehoahaz's* son *Joash*, so called in 2 Kings xiii. 9; but in the following verse called "*Jehoash*"; then, in verses 12, 13 and 14, "*Joash*", and, in verse 25, called both "*Jehoash*" and "*Joash*", while, in xiv. 1, his father, who in the last verse of the previous chapter is called "*Jehoahaz*", is called "*Joahaz*". Why all this bewildering confusion? Is this making matters so plain that "wayfaring men, yea fools, shall not err therein"? Isa. xxxv. 8.

We have, in English, two words which are very similar to each other, and therefore are often misused, "*O*" and "*Oh*". The former is simply vocative, and the latter is an exclamation of surprise, pain, sorrow, or desire.

As in other matters, so in this, the Revisers, being uncertain as to the right use of each, have erred in the use of both.

I give the Revisers credit for having endeavoured to write correctly; but it was beyond them, they could not do it. Simple as is the rule respecting "*O*" and "*Oh*", the Revisers being as frequently wrong as they are right when they had to employ either of the words, it is evident that their correct use was unknown to them.

Both "*O*" and "*Oh*" are correctly employed in Psa. xcv.; the former in verse 6, the latter in verse 7.

"O come, let us worship and bow down;
Let us kneel before the Lord our Maker."

There is "*O*" vocative.

"Oh that ye would hear his voice."

There is "*Oh*" expressive of desire, but not vocative.

The Revisers seem occasionally to have had glimpses of what is right respecting these words, and give us a flash of the truth; but it is only a flash; it goes out immediately, and all is again darkness.

Thrice they have corrected "*O*" to "*Oh*", but more than five times as frequently have they left "*O*" unaltered, though in every instance the sentence is expressive of some sentiment, feeling, passion, or desire.

Compare Prov. xxx. 13; Psa. ci. 2; and cxix. 97, which the Revisers have altered, with the following which they have not altered:

Psa. xxv. 17, 20; xxxvi. 10; xliii. 1, 3; lxi. 7; lxvii. 4; lxxiv. 19, 21; lxxxvi. 16; lxxxix. 47; xc. 14; cvi. 4; cix. 26; cxix. 8, 10.

Look also at Judges vi. 13, 15; there they have employed "*Oh*", although the expressions are only vocative.

"*Oh* my Lord", and "*Oh* Lord".

The inconsistency of the Revisers will be better seen if we compare passages in which the expressions are similar; e.g., Psa. vii. 9, with Psa. lxvii. 4; lxxiv. 21; and cxix. 10.

> "*Oh* let the wickedness of the wicked come to an end.

That is correct; the expression being one of desire; so also are the following passages expressions of desire, but the interjections, being vocative, are wrong.

> "*O* let the nations be glad and sing for joy."

> "*O* let not the oppressed return ashamed."

> "*O* let me not wander from thy commandments."

In my criticisms on the New Testament Revisers' errors, I have so fully discussed the error of using "*wilt*" for "*willest*", that I must refer my readers to that work for the reasons which justify my condemnation of the error.

In Esther v. 3, we have,

"What *wilt* thou, queen Esther?"

This should be,

"What *willest* thou, queen Esther?"

In Job xxxiv. 33, we have,

" Shall his recompense be as thou wilt?"

" As thou wilt " what? The sentence is not complete; "*wilt*" is only an auxiliary to another verb. The sentence should be,

" Shall his recompense be as thou *willest*?"

The Revisers' error of using "*if*" for "*whether*", "*though*" for "*if*"; and "*except*" for "*unless*" need not be criticized here; enough having been said on those matters also in ' *The Revisers' English*'. I will merely quote some of the passages in the Old Testament where the errors will be found.

"*If*", used incorrectly for "*whether*", will be found in Gen. viii. 8; Psa. xiv. 2; cxxxix. 24; Jer. ii. 10; v. 1; Lam. i. 12; and Mal. iii. 10: and yet in Cant. vii. 12; Joel ii. 14; and

Jonah iii. 9, the Revisers have corrected the error. But why there, and not elsewhere? Will they condescend to tell us?

"*Whether*" is used correctly in Gen. xviii. 21; xxxvii. 14; Ex. iv. 18; xxii. 8; Num. xiii. 18, 19, 20, and elsewhere.

"*Though*," used incorrectly for "*if*", will be found in Gen. xl. 10; Num. xviii. 27; 1 Sam. xx. 20; 2 Sam. iv. 6; Job. x. 19; Psa. xxxv. 14; lviii. 7; Obad. 16; and Zech. x. 6: and yet in Job. xxxix. 16, the Revisers have corrected the error. But why they selected that particular passage for correction, and left the rest, is probably known only to themselves; if, indeed, it is known to them. The error in Psa. lviii. 7, does not exist in the Authorised Version.

"*Except*", used incorrectly for "*unless*", will be found in Gen. xxxi. 42; xxxii. 26; xlii. 15; xliii. 3, 5, 10; xliv. 23, 26; Deut. xxxii. 30; Josh. vii. 12; 1 Sam. xxv. 34; 2 Sam. iii. 13; v. 6; 2 Kings iv. 24; Esther ii. 14; Psa. cxxvii. 1; Isa. i. 9; Dan. vi. 5; and Amos iii. 3. In

Prov. iv. 16, both words occur, the one wrong, the other right:

> "They sleep not, *except* [*unless*] they have done mischief;
> And their sleep is taken away, *unless* they cause some to fall."

The rule respecting these two words will be found in '*The Revisers' English*', p. 95, of the 2nd Edition. Briefly, it is this : "*except*" should be used in referring to persons or to things; and "*unless*", in referring to actions.

The word "*unless*" is used correctly in Psa. xxvii. 13; xciv. 17; cxix. 92, and elsewhere.

> "I had fainted, *unless* I had believed to see the goodness of the Lord
> In the land of the living."

> "*Unless* the Lord had been my help,
> My soul had soon dwelt in silence."

> "*Unless* thy law had been my delight,
> I should then have perished in mine affliction."

"*Except*" is used correctly in Dan. ii. 11; and iii. 28.

"There is none other that can show it before the king, *except* the gods whose dwelling is not with flesh."

"That they might not serve nor worship any god, *except* their own God."

Sometimes the Revisers are wrong as to facts. In their preface they say that the word "*its*" does not appear to have been introduced into any edition of the Bible before 1660.

More than twenty years ago I had a discussion with the late Dean Alford upon this matter; and if the Revisers will refer to my work, '*The Dean's English*', p. 70, 11th edition, they will read of the word "*its*" found in a Bible published in 1653.

In Prov. xxv. 20, the Revisers say,

"As vinegar upon *nitre*,
So is he that singeth songs to an heavy heart."

The entire force of the illustration is lost by the use of the word "*nitre*"—i.e., saltpetre—for, this salt produces no visible result of any kind on intermixture with vinegar.

The word "*nitre*" should probably have been "*natron*", i.e., crude carbonate of soda. Vinegar, upon being poured over natron, developes a copious froth, the hollowness and rapid subsidence of which are in keeping with the effect of the singing of songs to a heavy heart.

In Deut. viii. 9, we are told that Palestine is

"A land whose stones are iron, and out of whose hills thou mayest dig "*brass*."

But neither out of the hills of Palestine, nor out of any other hills can brass be dug. Brass is an alloy of copper and zinc, or of copper and tin, and does not exist as a natural product. This fact ought to have taught the Revisers that the word "*brass*" must be a mistranslation.

The Revisers are not at all "*horsey*", or they would not have made any mistake about bits and bridles. But thrice they speak of "*bridles*" where what are meant are "*bits*", e.g.;

"I will put my *bridle* in thy *lips*". 2 Kings xix. 28; and Isa. xxxvii. 29.

"A *bridle* that causeth to err shall be in the *jaws* of the peoples". Isa. xxx. 28.

In 2 Sam. viii. 1, the *bridle* is spoken of as being taken out of the *hand*, which is correct; but who ever heard of a "*bridle*" being in the "*lips*" or the "*jaws*" of any animal?

The '*Edinburgh Review*' remarked on Job xxxix. 25, "Even the horse is no longer allowed by the Revisers to snort 'Ha, Ha'; but is made, like human beings, to say 'Aha'".

In Isa. v. 29, we read,

"Their roaring shall be like a lion."

A roaring may be like *that of* a lion, but the roaring cannot be like a lion.

In Psa. ciii. 5, we read,

"Thy youth is renewed like the eagle."

A man's youth may be said to be renewed like the fabled renewal of the eagle's youth; and thus the passage stands in the Authorised Version; but how a portion of a man's existence can be like an eagle, let the Revisers explain.

. What do the Revisers mean us to understand when they say, in Psa. xcv. 7,

> "We are the *people* of his *pasture*, and the *sheep* of his *hand*."?

"*People*" do not "*pasture*", nor are "*sheep*" led by the "*hand*". Doubtless what the Psalmist meant, was,

> "We are the *sheep* of his *pasture*";

(which agrees with Psa. c. 3, "We are . . . . the sheep of his pasture";) and

> "We are the *people* of his *hand*";

(which agrees with Jer. xxxi. 32, "I took them by the hand to bring them out of the land of Egypt").

The Revisers' punctuation is, to say the least of it, peculiar. Who was Sarai Abram? and who was "*Sarai Abram's wife*"? In Gen. xii. 17, we read that

> "The Lord plagued Pharaoh and his house with great plagues because of *Sarai Abram's wife:*"

and, in Gen. xvi. 1, we read that

"*Sarai Abram's* wife bare him no children."

In Gen. iv. 2, we are told that Eve bore Cain's brother Abel twice!

"And *again* she bare his brother Abel."

Very strange! And here is something else very strange. The Revisers tell us that there can be two second times of doing the same thing. To me it seems to be an impossibility, even though God Himself is said to be the doer. See Isa. xi. 11;

> "It shall come to pass in that day, that the Lord shall set his hand *again the second time* to recover the remnant of his people."

Fortunately they have put a comma after the word "*old*" in Isa. lxiii. 11, or the reading would have been rather irreverent.

> "Then he remembered the days of old, Moses, and his people."

A comma in each of the previously quoted passages, viz. Gen. xii. 17; xvi. 1; iv. 2; and Isa. xi. 11; would have saved the Revisers from justly merited reproach.

P 2

In 2 Kings xix. 35, and Isa. xxxvii. 36, we read of "*dead* corpses". Are there, then, *live* corpses? The Revisers seem to have some horrible ideas.

Finally, why do the Revisers represent Solomon's beloved one as saying in Cant. ii. 5, and v. 8,

"I am sick of love",

when love is so absorbing her whole soul that she is sick of everything but love? It should be,

"I am sick *with* love";

as in Jer. xiv. 18, "sick with famine."

To be sick *of* a thing, is to be heartily tired of it, as I am of the Revisers' errors; and probably the Revisers will feel that they are sick of the *vexation* of my criticisms, and, in their own elegant language, will say,

"A stone heavy, and the sand weighty;
But a fool's *vexation* is heavier than *them* both." Prov. xxvii. 3.

"Heavier than *them*" are! Enough.

My task is done, and I lay down my pen. Is it with a sense of relief? Nay, rather with a sad and heavy heart; for I know but too well how golden an opportunity has been lost; the like of which may not occur again for generations.

Our English Bible, which to millions of the human race will for ever remain the standard of moral and religious truth, ought to have been made also the standard of all that is pure, and graceful, and noble, in our language. It is the Temple of Truth in whose solemn archives are kept the records of past ages, and the memorials of the infancy of our race. Therein are enshrined also all human experiences, the utterances of holy desire, the breathings of fervent hope, the expressions of unwavering faith, and the exulting songs of a nation's triumphs. Therein, too, are heard the sighs of the broken-hearted, the groans of the soul's agonies in its wrestlings with sin; and, coming up from the dungeon-depths of despair, the smothered cry of remorse from the self-condemned. But these are not the only voices: therein are heard also the prayers of the mighty minds that have moved heaven by their supplications; and therein are heard the lispings of the little ones that have taught us life's lessons of child-like trust. Moreover, therein above all is heard the voice of God!—heard in its mighty thunderings, heard in its awful holiness, heard in its yearning pity, and heard in its undying love. All these voices live and reverberate in this Temple of Truth, and thence are ever echoed along the long corridors of time for the world's instruction and admonition. Why then, when this sanctuary of all that the heart holds to be most sacred needed repair, did the Revisers "daub it with untempered mortar?"—Ezk. xiii. 11-15.

THE END.

www.ingramcontent.com/pod-product-compliance
Lightning Source LLC
Chambersburg PA
CBHW031727230426
43669CB00007B/273